A Table Full of Love

Skye McAlpine

A Table Full of Love

Recipes to
Comfort,
Seduce,
Celebrate
*& Everything
Else in Between*

BLOOMSBURY PUBLISHING

NEW YORK · LONDON · OXFORD · NEW DELHI · SYDNEY

CONTENTS

To Olga, my fairy godmother.
With all my love always.

*This symbol denotes a care package
recipe, which can be left on the
doorstep of anyone who might like it,
but which takes equally well to being
transported for any occasion.*

COMFORT

SEDUCE

NOURISH

SPOIL

COCOON

MENUS

Flour, sugar and cocoa cup measures are spooned and leveled.

Brown sugar measurements are firmly packed.

Other non-liquid cup measurements are loosely packed.

Where we have given measurements in cups and in metric weight, please use only one set of measurements.

Some thoughts on love and food

This is a book about love, the different kinds of love that permeate and underpin our world, that make life richer, more complex, at times more painful, often happier; the kinds of love that ultimately make life worth living. It's written in the language of food, so it's roast chicken with crisp, salty browned skin; bowls of thick soup, so creamy and rich by way of nourishing flavor that you can taste it with every fiber of your battered and bruised being. It's cookies, studded with bittersweet chocolate chunks, still chewy and slightly under-baked (deliciously so) at their center; and it's birthday cake, lots of birthday cake, because of all the things to cook for someone you love, birthday cake is the most joyous of them all.

Every cookbook at its heart is fundamentally a manual, a 'how-to' intended to help you with the practical business of cooking, and this book certainly is no exception, but the emphasis here is on *why* we cook as much as it is on *how* to do it. In the pages that follow, you'll find recipes to comfort, seduce, nourish and spoil your loved ones, as well as yourself; recipes to weave joy and delight into your everyday.

Life is busy and rushed, and cooking can often feel like something we *have* to do, a humdrum chore to add to the ever-growing list of other humdrum chores that is daily life: too easily and too often we find ourselves dreading having to make dinner, rather than looking forward to eating it. My hope in writing this book is to prompt you to *want* to cook more often, most especially for those people you most care about.

Above all, I hope this book will encourage you to cook not because you feel you should, but because doing so makes you that little bit happier. Because the act of quite simply making a plate of food for someone can reap the richest rewards: appreciation, friendship, sometimes admiration and even – on occasion – infatuation. Love. Because if there's one lesson I have learned in life, it's that food cooked with love begets more love.

And of all the friends I have made over the years, of all the relationships that I treasure and that make my life what it is, so many of those have come about over lunch, over dinner, or – best of all – over the kind of really good meal that starts off as lunch, lingers on through the afternoon and morphs happily into dinner. There's nowhere I would rather be than sitting at a table full of love.

Mostly, cooking is habit, a carousel of breakfast-lunch-dinner driven by the rhythm of our daily lives. It's just something we do, with little thought as to why (other than an instinctive need to satisfy hunger, of course), though often with much thought as to the what and the how. For me, it's something that has over the years come to be an immense source of comfort and pleasure. But I know that not everyone loves cooking... and certainly there are aspects of the mechanics and the process that I'm not too fond of myself. I loathe chopping, for example, and I'm hopeless at it; I don't much like peeling either, and I definitely don't enjoy dishwashing.

But at times, when my world is spinning out of control, it can be nice to have the excuse to use my hands and switch off from the turmoil, the gale howling around me. At such times, especially when we're feeling tired and down and like it's all too much, we might choose to buy something ready to eat from the store, or order in, rather than cook (and sometimes that's what I do); but somehow it's never quite the same as home-cooked food. If I'm honest, as much as I love a good takeout now and then, I quickly tire of ready to eat food if I have it too often.

I genuinely believe that chicken tastes better when I roast it myself rather than when I buy it from the rotisserie, for example: I smother the bird with butter, douse it in olive oil and lemon so the skin becomes really crisp and the meat tastes tender, salty and buttery. And, I guess, I'm greedy enough to think this is a worthwhile use of my time. That said, I'm also now old and wise enough to know that the whole roasting-your-own-chicken business will only take about five minutes of my time, ten at most, then the bird just sits in the oven doing its own thing, while I get on with my life happy in the comforting knowledge that a deeply soothing supper awaits me.

All of these – hunger, greed, a craving for the comforts of the homemade – are good, valid and highly practical reasons to cook, but in truth, none of them is really *why* I cook. Mostly, I cook because I enjoy how good it makes me feel to bring people together. I cook because I love the people I cook for, and food is perhaps how I best know to express that feeling. My happiest place is sitting round a long table filled with friends, old and new, eating and chattering, indulging in each other's company.

The real flavor of any dish will always equate to more than the simple sum of its raw ingredients: good food can't help but taste of the tangle of emotions and memories we collect over a lifetime of eating, cooking and being cooked for. And of all those emotions, the most prominent and ever recurring – that feeling we want to hold on to and the magic, intangible ingredient which has a way of making all food taste like you can't live without it – is love.

Today, the word 'love' is a sort of blanket term in which we bundle up everything from a taste for sweet potatoes ('I love them!' and indeed I do) to that tight squeezey feeling you get in your chest when your child first says 'Mama' ('I love you!' and more than you can ever imagine).

In my teens and twenties, I spent a lot of time thinking about love: I studied classics, first as an undergraduate degree and then, as my studies stretched on through the following decade, I embarked (possibly misguidedly, but that's another story) upon a masters degree and then a doctorate. My particular interest was ancient love poetry, most especially the works of the rather sexy Roman poet Ovid, but broadly I studied anything written about love in the centuries before the birth of Christ up until about the 1st Century AD.

Much of what I learned in those years – scansion, meter, vocabulary and so forth – I've now forgotten, but something that has stayed with me, and which still fascinates me, is the nuanced way in which the Greeks and the Romans understood love. In the constellation of the ancient world there are many kinds of love, each with its own name, like characters in a novel: there is *Eros* (lust), *Philia* (friendship), *Ludus* (flirtation), *Storge* (unconditional love), *Philautia* (self-love), *Pragma* (family love), *Mania* (obsessive love) and *Agape* (love for all things).

It is these different kinds of love that are the inspirations

and the foundations for this book, and that dictate its rhythm.
Just as it is love – in some shape or form – that dictates how
and why I cook, as well as why I love to cook.

Like leafing through the pages, faded and ever so slightly sticky,
of an old family photo album, each dish in this book takes me
on a meander through memories I might otherwise have long
lost. I can hear my mother's strict instructions to 'keep stirring,
keep stirring' whenever I make risotto; and the soft, purring
Irish lilt of my sweet friend Eileen's voice whenever I revisit
her recipe for raisin-studded brack cake infused with bitter,
floral-scented tea. This book is far more personal than anything
I have written before, and the recipes here are those that hold
the most sentimental value for me, largely because of the people
with whom I associate them.

In gathering together these recipes, I set out to compose
a culinary love letter to those people who matter to me the
most, and yet, through the process of writing this book, I have
learned a lot about myself too. Through each of the five
chapters, I can trace different iterations of myself, from who
I was to who I am: from my dating days to motherhood; from
carpet picnics in my college room to playing hostess with a
proper 'grown-up' kitchen; and from being lost to finding a way.

My hope is that in my story you will find echoes of your own
life – the highs and lows, the everyday, the meaningful and the
memorable – alongside recipes that go with them. As I look
back on this book in its entirety, I realize that, yes, this is a
book about love and food, but it is also a book about identity:
it's about me, about you, about who we are, and about who we
hope to be. And it's very much about what we're going to cook
and eat along the way.

Although its structure is a little unconventional, I hope you
will nonetheless find this book intuitive to use. The chapter
headings are not 'breakfast', 'lunch' and 'dinner', nor are they
'appetizers', 'entrées' or 'desserts', as you might expect; instead
the recipes are organized by mood and by sentiment.
I want to encourage you to pick the book up and choose just

one thing, anything, then cook it for someone you care about. You can of course do more, you can add side dishes to an entrée, you can make a big crisp salad to go with your roast or your casserole or your pasta. Make a dessert as well if you're looking for a full, well-rounded meal, or just make a dessert if that's what you crave and what makes you feel good (for me, it often does). But I want to insist that there is no need for more: above all, I would love for you to choose one thing, something hearty and filling, or something frivolous and sweet, anything, you name it, and just make it.

I believe it was Voltaire who said *le mieux est l'ennemi du bien:* 'the best is the enemy of the good'. I live out so much, too much really, of my life with that all-or-nothing voice ringing noisily in my head, the voice that stops me from doing something good because it's not everything, or the very best; because it's not perfect. It's the voice that kills off joy, supplanting it instead with guilt and the ugly entourage of uncomfortable feelings that always seem to come with guilt. Yet the one place I find that voice falls silent is in the kitchen, and maybe that's why I'm so happy there.

Ultimately, I truly believe that, when it comes to cooking, less is blissfully more. You can show someone you love them, you can bring them joy and touch their lives with one simple thing: and that's a great part of the magic of it. What matters is to cook *something*, rather than perhaps trying to make ever more, and ever more challenging, food, and then stumbling or losing heart along the way. I hope that is what you will do.

Lastly, I want to labor the point that the chapter motifs here are not intended in any way as dogma, but as gentle guides only. There is no one way to say 'I love you', just as there is no one single way to love. The recipes here reflect what I most love to eat, just as they paint a portrait of the people in my life I care most about.

I don't want you to feel that because I prescribe mac and cheese as a remedy for heartbreak, you shouldn't reserve it for your happiest days too. Because I do: I love mac and cheese pretty much whatever is going on in my life. Nor would I want you to think that because I give a recipe for tiramisù that feeds two, you shouldn't or can't scale it up when you're cooking for a crowd, or indeed scale it down to one when you're cooking just for you. I certainly do; and you must too. And yes, I wrote the Nourish chapter about feeding my two boys, but all the recipes there could equally serve to nurture and cherish those people you care for, no matter what their age or how they fit into your life. You must pick and choose these recipes as you like, and of course adapt as you desire and see fit. You must build your own language of love, one dish, one dessert, one meal at a time... and perhaps, just perhaps, a handful of the recipes here might come to be root words in that vocabulary. You might just begin to think of some of the recipes in the pages that follow as your own, and that would bring me the greatest pleasure of all.

With all my cookbooks, my goal is to make your workload lighter, not heavier. I believe that good food is much more about intention and thoughtfulness than it is about execution. Which is why the recipes you will find here are, above all, simple. Where there are shortcuts, I've taken them, and I'd urge you with almost evangelical fervor to do so too.

Some of the dishes in this book require so little by way of actual cooking that I feel almost abashed to pass them off as recipes. Yet, as it turns out, it's those dishes, the ones that involve the minimum number of pans (and associated dishwashing) and that offer what most closely resembles instant gratification, that tend to be my own favorites, the ones that I cook most often; so here they are. You will find lots of this kind of 'non-cooking cooking' here.

Mostly these are Italian flavors, some more or less canonical, often with a British something about them, and perhaps the occasional Antipodean intonation. I was born in London and grew up in Venice; now I live between the two cities and find myself married to a handsome Australian who has strong views about how to grill steak and what constitutes a proper pavlova. So my world is a hodgepodge of geographies, and my style of cooking in many ways – inevitably perhaps – looks that way too.

The one constant is that I always choose the path of least resistance: this is all do-able food, made with easily accessible (albeit sometimes seasonal) ingredients. And where, very occasionally, a little more effort is required, I promise you – hand on heart – it is well worth it.

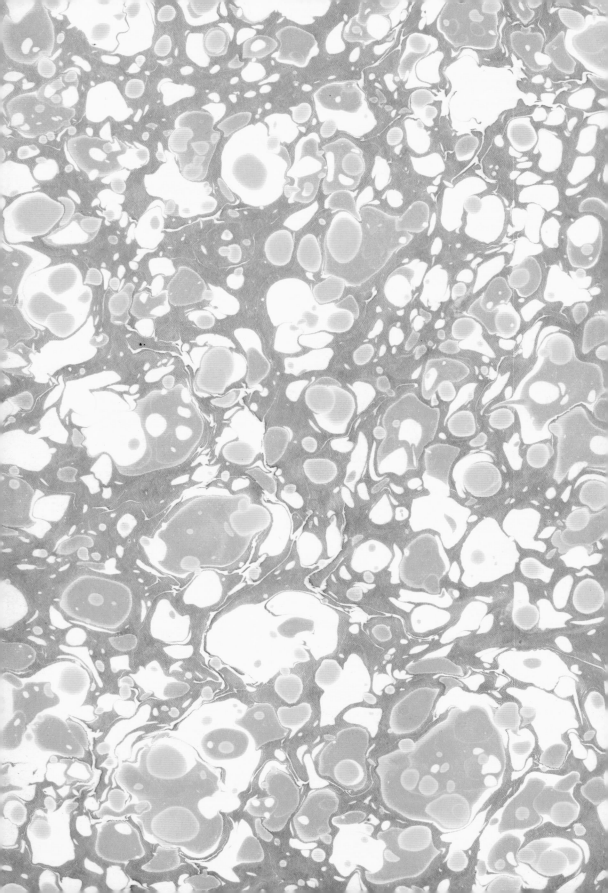

COMFORT

Some thoughts on friendship, and recipes for mending heartbreak

All books begin with the seed of an idea, something scribbled down in haste on the back of a cocktail napkin, maybe, or in the dog-eared pages of a notebook. This book started with the recipe for Sue's Magical Chicken Soup, in neat longhand on a piece of monogrammed notepaper torn from a hotel notepad. I could wax lyrical about how clear the broth is, or how Sue always uses a boiling chicken, not a roasting chicken (she's very specific about that). I could describe how you need to strain the broth four times to get it just right, and that therein lies its alchemy. But I won't, because for me that's not where the magic lies.

That soup takes me back to the time when my mother was ill in hospital with cancer, first one type and then another cancer, and the operations meant to make her better seemed only to make her worse. There came a point when the doctors insisted that if she was to live, she must eat. We tried everything: the high-calorie milkshake that the kindly nurse with the short hair recommended; toast with butter, peanut butter, with preserves; just toast; ice cream; pasta; rice. Anything. Everything.

The only food she would touch was Sue's chicken soup. They go back a long way, my mother and Sue: they were at school together, where they wore the same thick, itchy woollen stockings, and navy ribbons in their hair, and shared a desk in class. They have drifted in and out of each other's lives for decades, in that way that you do when you've known someone for longer than you can remember not knowing them.

When my mother was sick, each day Sue made a batch of soup and drove to the hospital to drop it off at the front desk; the next day she would return, collect the empty container, and drop off more soup. One spoonful at a time, my mother began to eat: just a very little to start with, then a little more, but only really to avoid disappointing Sue. Slowly, she began eating other things, a morsel of this and a mouthful of that. Then, one day, she said she thought she felt hungry.

It's been eight years now, and we still talk about the healing powers of Sue's chicken soup. My mother credits it with saving her life and I credit it with saving one of the most precious parts of mine. We call it Sue's-magical-chicken-soup, just like that, as if it were a single polysyllabic word. While I am prone to excitable hyperbole as much as the next person, I know that in this case there is no exaggeration. Sue's soup was more than chicken and celery and carrot; it was memories, hope, the taste of home, the taste of a world beyond a hospital bed. It was Sue's precious time, her care and her love.

Beyond soup, this chapter contains recipes for when the world looks bleak. This is food to lift the spirits, to heal what's broken, to stitch back together what's come undone. These are recipes for bumps in the road, for days when you've risen to the challenge and found that doing so took all you had to give.

Can we right the world's wrongs by making a pie or baking a cake? Maybe not. Maybe. 'Comfort' is a word much bandied about to describe food, often the sort of homey, butter-laden dish with a touch of the nursery about it that I so love. But comfort means different things for each of us. To you, it might taste of melted Parmesan, coconut milk, or eye-wateringly hot chiles. To my husband, it tastes like lamingtons, those squares of fluffy white sponge cake dipped in chocolate glacé icing and rolled in snowy shredded coconut. For me, there's something inexplicably comforting about canned tomato soup. It takes me back to childhood, to Sunday nights when the blues washed in like a tidal wave and my mother used to occasionally – and as a special treat – make me a mug (always a mug) of Heinz Cream of Tomato Soup, mixing the soup with half a can of water and half a can of milk to make it extra-creamy. Years later, when recovering from the physical trauma of the births of both my sons, canned tomato soup was what I craved above all else.

So, you might call the collection of recipes in the pages that follow my favorite comfort foods. There's soup (chicken and creamy tomato); there's chicken pie, and mac and cheese; there's the chocolate coconut cake that reminds me of childhood summer vacations, and the ice cream I've been known to eat an entire pint of in one sitting (more than once).

But this chapter isn't about comfort food, so much as comfort*ing*. It's about cooking as a way to care for those you love, especially when they're struggling to care for themselves. This might translate to simply making a cup of tea and a plate of thick, hot buttered toast. Or it might be laying on roast chicken with all the sides, followed by apple crumble with lashings of cream. In practical terms, cooking for comfort can look like a dish you drop off on the doorstep for someone to enjoy later, in their own time and space: a pie perhaps, wrapped

in foil ready to warm in the oven later, or a dessert, ideally something that will keep in the fridge or freezer for a few days. Not having to worry about cooking can be a huge comfort in times of crisis. Sometimes, however, the most comforting thing of all is to share a meal: to sit down with those you love, to envelop yourself in the warmth of their world, so that – for an evening, or for as long as Sunday brunch lasts – you can escape the woes that haunt yours. Sometimes the most comforting food of all is the kind that comes with a dear friend's advice and the chance to talk things over and over... and over again.

For better or for worse, real life is filled with moments that call for comfort cooking: there are tough days, there are the blues, there is heartbreak, there is illness and disappointment and bereavement. While it can be painful to dwell on this side of life, for each of these moments of deep darkness there is also respite in lunch, dinner, a pan of warm pie straight out of the oven, a good hunk of cake.

The pandemic-plagued years of 2020 and 2021 were filled with comfort cooking. Chimamanda Ngozi Adichie said 'grief is about language, the failure of language and the grasping for language'. How true that is. When those I love hurt, it is the helplessness, that crippling feeling of ineptitude that overcomes me, that hideous, painful emptiness that scratches on the sides of my stomach as in vain I reach for the right words. Of course, what no one ever tells you is that when the world crumbles, there are no 'right' words, there are just words. Cooking is the best way I have found to gently, silently say 'I love you', 'I'm here', 'I understand' or, 'I can't understand but I wish I could', to say it all and to say none of it at all. If a photograph speaks a thousand words, a steaming mug of Sue's chicken soup says only a few, but each more perfect and eloquent than anything spoken out loud could ever sound.

The thing about comfort food and comfort cooking is that, ultimately, it's a reciprocal business. We all know that food can offer us solace as well as nourishment. But I've also come to learn that there's as much comfort to be found in cooking for someone as there is in being cooked for. And that is perhaps the most important message of all. The recipes that follow are for hard times; my hope is that they'll help you just as, now and then, they've helped me.

Sue's Magical Chicken Soup

🎁 *Store in paper soup cups (I buy mine in bulk online) or airtight containers in the fridge for two or three days and reheat as needed. It also freezes well.*

Sue calls this 'Jewish penicillin' and it's true there's no other food I know that can heal the body or the soul quite like this chicken soup. The recipe is for a clear, clean broth, the kind of delicate soup our bodies crave when they're at their weakest. Don't waste the chicken meat, however: you can shred it into salads or pies (see pages 44, 47 and 286), or quite simply eat it up in a sandwich, with lashings of butter, peppery mustard and perhaps a few salad leaves. Or you can shred the meat and toss it back into the soup along with some cooked tiny pasta, if you feel like something a little more substantial to eat.

HANDS ON TIME:
20 minutes
HANDS OFF TIME:
2 hours on the stove;
5 hours cooling;
overnight in the fridge
SERVES 6

4 celery stalks
2 leeks
3 carrots
2 onions
3–4 chicken bouillon cubes
1 boiling chicken, cut into
    4 pieces
large bunch of parsley

Fill a large, deep saucepan with water, set over a high heat and bring to a boil. Meanwhile, roughly chop the vegetables into chunks.

When the water begins to gallop, crumble in 2 of the bouillon cubes, then add the chicken, vegetables and parsley. Cover the pan, reduce the heat and let the soup simmer for 2 hours.

Now add 1–2 more bouillon cubes to taste and take the pan off the heat.

Strain the soup through a fine-meshed strainer and remove the chicken (see recipe introduction) and vegetables, so you are left with a clear broth. Strain again through the fine-meshed strainer a further 3 times.

Cool to room temperature, then cover and set in the fridge to chill overnight.

Scrape off the layer of fat that has formed on top of the soup, then reheat it gently before serving warm.

Maria's Many Cheese Tiropita

🎁 *Prepare in a baking pan and cover with reusable food wrap. This will keep in the fridge for up to two days, or will freeze nicely. It is delicious at room temperature, or reheated gently in the oven.*

It was in the very first lockdown, that surreal, happy-sad spring of 2020, that the intense craving for Maria's cheese-laden pie first really beset me. I badgered her for the recipe, which, barely adapted, sits here on the page in front of you. Maria uses Kefalograviera cheese, which hails from Greece, but can be a little tricky to find in the US (though it is available online and in specialty shops, and if you can get your hands on it, tastes almost like burnt caramel). Instead I have replaced the Kefalograviera with grated mozzarella, which in no way resembles the milky white cheese we think of as mozzarella in Italy, but does melt beautifully, and is very easy to source. I'm sure it's utterly uncanonical and I hope that Maria will forgive me. The pie is totally delicious – and, like Maria, gloriously joyful – whichever cheese you choose to make it with.

HANDS ON TIME:
20 minutes
HANDS OFF TIME:
45 minutes in the oven
SERVES 6

5 eggs
2½ cups grated mozzarella
  cheese
2½ cups grated Cheddar
  cheese
2 cups crumbled feta
  cheese
1 cup plain whole milk
  Greek yogurt
3 tbsp olive oil, or
  vegetable oil
10oz (about 7 sheets)
  phyllo pastry
7 tbsp whole milk

Heat the oven to 350°F.

Lightly beat 3 eggs together in a large mixing bowl. Add the grated cheeses, feta cheese and yogurt and mix together with a wooden spoon.

Brush a 13 x 9-inch baking dish with olive oil. Line the dish with 2 sheets of phyllo pastry, letting them cover the sides of the dish. Brush with olive oil again. Line with 2 more sheets and brush with olive oil. Spread the cheese filling evenly over the pastry layer. Layer 2 more phyllo sheets on top and brush with oil. Lay a last sheet of pastry over the top and brush with oil for a final time.

Cut the tiropita into squares (cutting only part of the way through, not all the way down through the bottom layer of pastry). Whisk the last 2 eggs together with the milk (I do this in the same mixing bowl as the cheese filling to save on dishwashing), then pour the eggy mixture over the pie.

Set in the oven and bake for 45 minutes until crisp and golden brown. Cover with foil after 30 minutes, if it looks like it's crisping too much.

Serve warm, with a crisp green salad or a dish of juicy tomatoes steeped in olive oil and adorned with nothing but a few fragrant basil leaves and thin slivers of sweet red onion.

Beet, Walnut and Gorgonzola Tart

🎁 Bundle up in a cake box (I buy these in bulk online), or wrap up in reusable food wrap. This keeps in the fridge, or even just somewhere cool, for up to two days.

I have lost count of how many times, over the years, I have made this, yet every time it surprises me by how inexplicably good it is. It's a crowd pleaser: something about the earthiness of the beets together with the buttery pastry and the rich blue cheese. By no means an innovative flavor combination, but a comfortingly classic one.

The walnuts are not essential, but frankly awfully good, as they add just a dash of waxy crumble, a little crunch, to the filling. Even those who profess not to enjoy blue cheese always seem to relish this tart. You can serve it either warm straight from the oven, or it's equally good at room temperature, which makes it ideal for cooking in advance or for dropping off on friends' doorsteps in times of need (or indeed, celebration too; it's my go-to for dinner parties and birthday parties).

As for the beets, I tend to use the kind you can buy vacuum-packed and ready-cooked (I keep packages of this lingering in the bottom of my fridge, so I can easily and with little notice make either this tart or the salad on page 112). But, if you prefer and have the time, you could of course roast your own: heat the oven to 350°F, wash the beets and remove the leaves, but keep 1 inch or so of the stalk and the root intact, then put in a roasting pan, drizzle with olive oil and salt and roast for about 45 minutes, or until you can inter a dinner knife into the root and feel no resistance. Once cool, rub off the skin with paper towels and then follow the recipe as written.

HANDS ON TIME:
10 minutes
HANDS OFF TIME:
35 minutes in the oven
SERVES 4-6

1 store-bought refrigerated
    pie crust (from a 14.1-oz
    package)
4 medium cooked beets
    (about 10oz)
1½ cups crumbled
    Gorgonzola cheese
handful of walnut pieces
1 tbsp olive oil
flaky sea salt and freshly
    ground black pepper

Heat the oven to 350°F.

Drape the pastry over a 9-inch loose-bottomed tart pan. Press the pastry into the pan's nooks and crannies and trim away any excess around the top. Pierce the bottom of the tart all over with a fork, then cover with parchment paper, fill with baking beans and set in the oven to blind-bake for 20 minutes until the pastry is lightly golden at the edges. Remove the parchment paper and the beans and set the pan back in the oven to bake for a further 5 minutes until the pastry at the base feels dry to the touch.

Slice the beets into rounds 1½–2 inches thick and arrange the slices in the tart crust in a single layer, slightly overlapping. Scatter over the Gorgonzola and walnuts, drizzle over the olive oil and season with a little salt and pepper. Bake in the oven for 10 minutes, until the cheese is completely melted and the edges of the tart are golden. Serve warm or at room temperature.

Deeply Comforting Tomato Soup

🎁 *Package up in paper soup cups or airtight containers. This will keep in the fridge for up to three days, or freezes happily for much longer.*

It's the intense creaminess of this tomato soup that is so devilishly good, like balm – warming and mellow – for the soul. It's surprising really, given that there is no cream in the recipe: just tomatoes and broth, a dash of sugar and a splash of sweet balsamic vinegar (the very best kind you can get your hands on). But nonetheless, somehow and by some kind of culinary magic, all together it tastes like cream. I use cherry tomatoes because I find them sweeter and less watery than the larger variety, most especially if – like me – you're buying them from the supermarket. You will find that as much as you blend the soup, you will still be able to taste the tiny seeds in it; these don't bother me, in fact I rather enjoy the singularly homemade taste of something imperfectly made with fresh ingredients. However, if you prefer your soup silky-smooth, you can of course strain out the seeds by passing the soup through a strainer before warming and serving it. Because I most crave this soup when I crave comfort, I tend to enjoy it best served piping hot with hot buttered toast or chunks of crusty bread (ideally laced with salty black Marmite); but in truth, this is equally delicious served chilled on a warm summer's day (or evening), with a dollop of crème fraîche or sour cream, a smattering of freshly ground black pepper and a few sweet basil leaves. One last important tip: whatever tomatoes you choose to go with, make sure *not* to store them in the fridge, instead always keep them at room temperature (I keep mine in a large dish on the sideboard in our kitchen): this works miracles for their flavor and, if it's not something you're doing already, it will change your life.

HANDS ON TIME:
10 minutes
HANDS OFF TIME:
35 minutes cooking
SERVES 4-6

2 tbsp salted butter
1 onion, chopped
6¾ cups cherry tomatoes
2 tbsp balsamic vinegar
2 tsp granulated sugar
3⅓ cups vegetable broth
flaky sea salt and freshly
    ground black pepper
olive oil, to serve (optional)

Melt the butter in a large saucepan over a medium heat. Add the onion and a generous pinch of salt, then fry gently for 3–5 minutes until the onion turns soft and translucent.

Add the tomatoes – whole is fine, no need to halve or chop them unless you are using larger tomatoes – along with the balsamic and sugar, then cover with the broth.

Bring everything to a boil, then reduce the heat and let simmer gently for 30 minutes, until the tomatoes have broken down (or at the very least feel deeply squishable).

Take the pan off the heat and use a hand blender to blitz the soup until smooth. Season to taste with salt and pepper and serve warm, with a glug of olive oil if you like (or you could equally well leave it to cool and serve chilled, see recipe introduction).

Saffron and Lemon Risotto

There is something so deeply comforting about risotto: the ritual of making it that forces you to hover over the pan, stirring slowly, mindlessly, for as long as the rice takes to be ready; that seductive smell of onion softening gently on the stove; the sheer quantities of butter and cheese that can't help but make things better; and that warm feeling on the inside I always get from eating it. This recipe is an adaptation of the buttery yellow saffron risotto my mother used to make for me as a child; it's not better than hers – no risotto is – but the touch of lemon makes it taste like the promise of summer and hope, something I most especially appreciate on darker days.

HANDS ON TIME:

30 minutes

SERVES 4

2 tbsp olive oil

1 onion, finely chopped

7 cups vegetable broth

1 tsp saffron strands

1¾ cups arborio rice

7 tbsp white wine

1 lemon

2 tbsp salted butter

⅓ cup grated Parmesan cheese, plus more (optional) to serve

flaky sea salt and freshly ground black pepper

Heat the oil in a heavy-based saucepan over a medium heat. Add the chopped onion and a pinch of salt, then fry gently for 3–5 minutes, until soft and translucent.

In a second saucepan, bring the broth to a boil over a medium heat.

Use a mortar and pestle to grind the saffron and a pinch of salt into a fine powder; this will give the risotto a more even color, but doesn't affect the taste, so feel free to skip this step if you prefer and add the strands as is.

Add the rice to the onion, increase the heat to high and cook for 3 minutes or so, until the rice begins to crackle softly and feels as though it's just starting to stick to the base of the pan. Now pour in the white wine and stir constantly for 2–3 minutes, until the rice has absorbed all the liquid.

Reduce the heat to medium and gradually add the hot broth, a ladleful at a time. Stir the rice continuously and wait until the liquid has been completely absorbed before adding each splash of broth. You want to keep the wet rice moving so that it cooks evenly through the risotto. Keep going in this manner for 15–20 minutes, until the rice is plump and tender but still firm at its center. You may not need all the broth.

Grate in the zest of the lemon and squeeze in its juice. Add the saffron (either in powdered form or in strands) and stir well until the risotto turns a deep yellow color. Just before taking the pan off the heat, stir in the butter and Parmesan. Add salt and pepper to taste and give it a last stir before serving piping hot, with more Parmesan, if you like.

Baked Fennel and Burrata Gratin

🎀 *Prepare in a baking dish and cover with reusable food wrap. Either pre-bake it so it only needs reheating in the oven, or prepare it up to the point of baking and drop off with cooking instructions. This keeps in the fridge for two days, or freezes well.*

You could make this with mozzarella instead of the burrata, but then you would miss out on that inimitably and indulgently creamy flavor you achieve only with burrata. And that, frankly, would be a shame. I love this: I love the subtle sweetness of the tender fennel, the heady richness of the cheese and the crisp golden breadcrumbs on top. I also love that it's so exquisitely simple to make: just a matter of interleaving slices of fennel with cheese and baking under a blanket of golden crumbs. I always add thyme because it gives an extra layer of flavor and goes so well with the fennel, but you could substitute herbs as you like: basil, mint, parsley and so forth. I sort of think of this dish as a summery *melanzane alla Parmigiana* (see page 176): it's lighter and more delicate, but still has that slightly stodgy, gloriously comforting quality that is the hallmark of any good cheesy casserole. It also is one of those dishes you can enjoy as an entrée, perhaps with a rice or lentil salad on the side: toss the grains with olive oil, herbs and perhaps some cherry tomatoes and/or capers or olives; something like the rice salad or the chickpea salad at pages 278 and 277 would be perfect. Or you can serve smaller portions of the cheesy gratin with anything from roast chicken to grilled fish, as you would a *pommes dauphinoise*.

HANDS ON TIME:
10 minutes
HANDS OFF TIME:
45 minutes in the oven
SERVES 4-6 as a main course, or **6-8** as a side dish

2 large fennel bulbs, trimmed (total weight about 1¼lbs)
10oz burrata
small bunch of thyme
1 cup heavy cream
generous ¾ cup panko breadcrumbs
scant ½ cup grated Parmesan cheese
2 tbsp salted butter
flaky sea salt and freshly ground black pepper

Heat the oven to 400°F.

Slice the fennel into ½-inch thick slivers. Arrange half in an ovenproof dish. Tear half the burrata into small pieces and dot it here and there over the fennel. Sprinkle over half the thyme and season with salt and pepper. Now add a second layer of fennel to the dish and top with the last of the burrata and thyme. Season again with a dash of salt and a good grinding of black pepper. Drizzle the cream over the fennel and burrata.

Now, combine the breadcrumbs and Parmesan in a small mixing bowl and scatter over the top of the dish. Slice the butter into small pieces and dot them here and there over the gratin.

Cover with foil and bake in the oven for 25 minutes, then remove the foil and bake for a further 20 minutes until golden all over.

Pumpkin and Mascarpone Flan

⌘ Bake, then cover with reusable food wrap. This will keep happily in the fridge for two or three days and is delicious both eaten at room temperature, or warmed up by the slice in the microwave.

I first ate this dish – or a version of it – in an unassuming little trattoria in Venice rather aptly called La Zucca or 'The Pumpkin'. The flan – wibbly-wobbly and exquisitely creamy – was so good that I, almost by return, set about trying to recreate it at home, and after a number of more or less successful attempts have settled on this recipe, which I can only describe as the culinary equivalent of wrapping yourself in a soft cashmere blanket. It tastes luxuriously comforting: everything about this dish, each buttery mouthful, tastes like nursery food in the most nostalgic and idyllic sense of the word.

The texture rather resembles that of a baked custard, but it's not a dessert; instead, infused with aromatic sage and laced with velvety mascarpone, like all dishes that involve sweet-scented pumpkin it falls into that happy space that is neither entirely savory nor quite dessert-sweet.

While the recipe here is for pumpkin, you can also make this with butternut squash: for ease I always buy the kind that comes peeled and diced in a bag. And while this really is at its peak deliciousness when warm from the oven, rather like quiche, it is also awfully good served at room temperature.

The flan itself is so rich that you really need little to go with it: perhaps some grilled vegetables on the side, some lentils or rice if you like and feel the need; or quite simply just have a large slice with a crisp green salad. I like to serve it whole on a dish, which shows to its best the gentle soft-set wobble.

HANDS ON TIME:
15 minutes
HANDS OFF TIME:
60–75 minutes in the oven;
15 minutes cooling
SERVES 6-8

1½lbs peeled and seeded
    pumpkin or butternut
    squash
handful of sage leaves
3 tbsp olive oil
2 tbsp salted butter,
    softened, plus more
    for the mold
1¾ cups mascarpone
5 eggs, lightly beaten
generous ¾ cup grated
    Parmesan cheese
2 tbsp white breadcrumbs
flaky sea salt and freshly
    ground black pepper

Heat the oven to 350°F.

Chop the pumpkin or squash into 1½–2 inch pieces (you should have approximately 5½ cups) and toss them into a roasting pan with the sage leaves. Drizzle with the olive oil and roast for 30–40 minutes until tender. Blend the cooked pumpkin or squash and crisp sage leaves with the butter in a food processor and season generously with salt and pepper.

Now add the mascarpone, eggs and Parmesan and blitz again until smooth.

Butter a 10½-inch (approximately 2¾ quarts) flan mold or ovenproof dish and sprinkle in the breadcrumbs; rotate the dish to ensure the layer of crumbs and butter is even, then tip out any excess crumbs. Pour in the pumpkin mixture and put in a deep roasting pan half-filled with hot water. I find it easiest to put the mold in the larger pan in the oven, then pour in the hot water around it, rather than trying to carry it smoothly to the oven already filled.

Cook for 30–35 minutes, until the flan is very lightly golden on top and feels almost firm to the touch; it should still be a little bit wobbly in the middle. Let cool for 15 minutes, then turn it out on to a plate and serve warm, or leave to cool a little more and eat at room temperature.

Soul-Soothing Roast Chicken

✠ *There are few things so satisfying or as reassuring as roast chicken. Wrap cooked and whole in foil, with the bird either in some kind of baking dish or just as is. This will keep in the fridge for two or three days and can be eaten at room temperature, either with salad or other vegetables, or in sandwiches, pies or salads (see pages 47, 286 and 44).*

My quest for the perfect roast chicken – golden, crisp salty skin, but the breast still plump and juicy – has been a lifelong pursuit, and this recipe is the closest I have come to it. The method, where you roast the bird first in a very, very hot oven and then let it rest in there with the door ajar for a good quarter of an hour before serving, comes to me from our local butcher Jack, at The Butcher's Table, who in turn takes his inspiration from Lindsey Bareham. It works a treat, and, since first trying to roast chicken this way, I'm firmly never going back to doing it any other which way. It may seem excessive to add both butter and olive oil, but the butter under the skin is what keeps the breast tender and imbues it with that exquisite flavor, while the drizzle of olive oil and flaky salt is what turns the skin golden, crisping it to perfection. It goes without saying that the quality of the bird you start with makes a big difference to the end result, so buy the best chicken you can.

HANDS ON TIME:
10 minutes
HANDS OFF TIME:
60–70 minutes in the oven;
15 minutes resting
SERVES 4 generously

1 x 3½lb chicken
5 tbsp salted butter,
    softened
3–4 tbsp olive oil
1 lemon
small bunch of rosemary
flaky sea salt and freshly
    ground black pepper

Heat the oven to 425°F.

Rest the chicken breast-side up in a roasting pan and use your fingers to gently lift up the flaps of skin over the breast and press the butter in there. Use your fingers to massage it, so as to get the butter as far in and as evenly distributed as possible without tearing the skin. Drizzle the oil over the skin and squeeze over the juice of the lemon, then stuff the 2 lemon halves inside the bird's cavity along with the rosemary. Sprinkle salt generously over the top of the chicken and give it a good grinding of black pepper.

Roast in the very hot oven for 30 minutes, then reduce the heat to 350°F and roast for a further 30–40 minutes. To test if the chicken is cooked, insert a knife into the thickest part (I usually go into the thigh, right by the crease of the leg) and see if the juices run clear. If so, turn the oven off and set the bird back in there, leaving it to rest, but keeping the door ajar, for 15 minutes before carving.

Just before serving, pour some of the buttery, fatty juices in the pan over the meat for extra flavor and to moisten it that little bit more.

A Very Good Chicken Salad

🎁 *Make a big batch of this and package it up in an airtight container (or a large mixing bowl covered with reusable food wrap). It will keep in the fridge for up to two days.*

This is a magnificent way to repurpose leftover roast chicken: it's also such a good dish that I have, more than once, found myself in the position of roasting a chicken for the sole purpose of making salad out of it. In fact, more often than not, if I'm roasting a chicken, I'll put a second bird in the oven at the same time so that I can make good use of it in sandwiches, pie (see overleaf) or – most frequently – in this delicately spiced, fresh-tasting, yogurt-y salad. When in season, I use fresh garden peas for this, but they categorically must be sharp-green, sweet-tasting peas, not dull and floury old-timers. When they are out of season (or if I can't get my hands on good fresh peas), I use frozen peas and lightly blanch them in salted water before adding, cooled, to the salad.

HANDS ON TIME:

10 minutes

SERVES 4

generous 1¾ cups
    plain whole milk
    Greek yogurt
2 tbsp za'atar
leaves from a small bunch
    of mint, finely chopped
3–4 tbsp olive oil
2½ cups shredded cooked
    chicken
¾ cup fresh garden peas
    (or see recipe
    introduction)
1 small fennel bulb, thinly
    sliced
flaky sea salt and freshly
    ground black pepper

In a large bowl, mix together the yogurt, za'atar, mint and olive oil.

Add the shredded chicken, peas and fennel, then toss gently until all is combined. Season to taste with salt and pepper before serving.

Petra's Creamy Saffron Chicken Pie

⌘ *Bake in an enamel roasting tray and cover with reusable food wrap. This pie can be reheated on the same day it is baked, or will freeze well.*

The first time I had pie like this, with a creamy, soupy underbelly and crumpled flashes of fine golden crisp phyllo pastry on top, was when Petra cooked it for me. It was a bitterly cold December day and we were at Petra's home in the Highlands for lunch. The skies were piercing blue-bright and almost indescribably beautiful, but I would be lying if I said that it wasn't brutally cold: I cannot tell you how wonderful it felt to come in from the brisk outdoors to a plate of this.

The saffron in the sauce is my own addition and you can of course leave it out if you prefer, or don't have any to hand, but I love the warmth of flavor and color it gives. You could also throw in some crumbled cooked chestnuts (vacuum-packed) or a few cooked vegetables, if you like.

Petra serves her chicken pie with buttered peas on the side, and I must say that buttered mashed potatoes laced with tart preserved lemons (see page 55) alongside it is a treat too. Alternatively, for ease, a salad – perhaps some red wine-hued endive leaves or other bitter winter leaves, lightly dressed – works well.

HANDS ON TIME:

35 minutes

HANDS OFF TIME:

30–35 minutes in the oven

SERVES 6

2 tbsp salted butter

2 leeks

6oz pancetta, cubed

4½ cups shredded cooked
  chicken

1 heaping tbsp all-purpose
  flour

scant 1 cup chicken broth

⅔ cup heavy cream

½ cup white wine

½ tsp saffron strands

4 sheets of phyllo pastry
  (approximately 15 x
  12 inches)

2–3 tbsp olive or
  vegetable oil

flaky sea salt and freshly
  ground black pepper

Heat the oven to 400°F.

Melt the butter in a large frying pan over a medium-high heat. Trim the leeks and slice into 1-inch chunks. Toss the leeks in the pan and cook for 5 minutes or so, until they soften and brown at the edges. Now add the pancetta (you should have about 1 cup of cubes) and fry gently for a further 5 minutes, until cooked through.

Toss the shredded chicken in the flour so that the pieces are lightly coated. Add the floured chicken to the pan and give it all a good stir. Pour in the broth, cream, wine and saffron strands. Bring to a boil, then reduce the heat and let the sauce bubble for 4–5 minutes until it thickens; it should look like a rich gravy. Season to taste.

Take off the heat and spoon the chicken and its yellow sauce into a 11 x 7-inch ovenproof pie dish (or, as long as the handle is ovenproof, you can bake the pie in the pan you cooked the chicken in, to save on dishwashing).

Spread the phyllo sheets out on a work surface, fold them in half and trim the folded edge to make a square shape. This doesn't need to be very precise: a rough square will do. Lightly brush the sheets of phyllo with the oil, then use a pair of scissors to cut across each diagonal of the layered sheets of pastry to make 4 triangles from each layer. You should have 32 triangles in all. Loosely scrunch up each oiled pastry triangle and arrange on top of the filling, until the pie is completely covered. It might seem like a palaver to cut the pastry into little triangles, but they look so appetizing atop the pie and make it much easier to slice through than whole scrunched-up sheets of crisp phyllo.

Bake in the oven for 30–35 minutes until the pastry is crisp and golden and the filling is bubbling hot. Serve warm with whatever veggies you fancy on the side.

Elle's Mac and Cheese

⊞ *Pile the pasta into a baking dish and cover with reusable food wrap. You can either pre-bake it so all the recipient needs to do is reheat it in the oven, or you can prepare it up until the point where you bake the macaroni and drop off with cooking instructions. It keeps in the fridge for two or three days, or freezes well.*

I've come to the exquisitely comforting joys of mac and cheese late in life. And it was Elle, with her pans of bubbling melted cheese and perfectly cooked pasta, who introduced me to this great life pleasure. The recipe here is largely Elle's (who in turn, I believe, inherited it from her grandmother): the pasta is cooked *al dente*, so still has texture and bite to it rather than appearing on your plate as a mound of mush, while the sauce is laced with a generous dash of paprika. You can't taste the spice really, not in any distinct or discernible way, but it gives a moreish-ness to the rich cheese sauce as well as an irresistibly golden color.

My only improvisation to Elle's original recipe is the addition of evaporated milk to the cheese sauce: this is a tip borrowed from Nigella Lawson's book *Christmas* (a gem of a cookery book that I turn to year-round in spite of its title). The combination of whole milk with just a splash of the evaporated kind (so creamy and rich in flavor) gives the sauce that quasi-plastic quality, as Nigella describes it, which is somehow just what you want for this kind of nostalgic dish that sits somewhere between nursery food and so-bad-that-it's-unbelievably-good food.

This is one of those dishes that freezes beautifully, so you can drop off food for someone to enjoy later without worrying; they will always find a good use for it.

5 cups macaroni or
  elbow pasta
6 tbsp salted butter
½ cup all-purpose flour
1 cup evaporated milk
scant 3 cups whole milk
3 cups grated Cheddar
  cheese
2 tsp paprika
⅔ cup grated Parmesan
  cheese
flaky sea salt and freshly
  ground black pepper

Heat the oven to 425°F.

Bring a large saucepan of generously salted water to a boil. When the water begins to gallop, add the pasta and cook very *al dente*, following the package instructions. You want the pasta on the slightly undercooked side, as it will cook again when you bake it in the oven. When the pasta is ready, drain the water, toss the macaroni back into the saucepan and set to one side.

Meanwhile, get on with the cheese sauce: in a medium saucepan, gently melt the butter over a low heat, then add the flour and keep stirring until you have a thick paste. Now, add the evaporated milk and the whole milk, little by little and stirring vigorously all the while so that lumps don't form: if you do get a few lumps (I always do), just stir vigorously until they've dissolved before adding more milk. When you have a sauce that resembles the consistency of lightly whipped cream, add the Cheddar and stir until combined and the cheese is largely melted. Take the pan off the heat, stir in the paprika and season to taste with salt and pepper.

Add the cheese sauce to the cooked pasta and toss together so everything is coated in exquisite cheesiness. Spoon the cheesy pasta into an ovenproof dish (I use an oval dish roughly 14 x 10 inches, or if I'm dropping a pan off, I typically spoon the macaroni into a rectangular roasting pan). Sprinkle the Parmesan over the top and set the dish in the oven for 20 minutes, until golden all over and bubbling hot. Serve warm, either as is, or with a crisp green salad on the side.

Buttery Mashed Potatoes
with Preserved Lemon

✽ *Pile into an airtight container and drop off with instructions to reheat gently in a pan on the stove (with a dash of extra olive oil and/or butter), or to microwave until warm. This will keep happily in the fridge for two or three days.*

There is something ever-comforting about the humble potato, most especially when mashed into a cloud of fluffy, starchy, buttery warmth. You will find that the method below calls for you to leave the skins on, so you end up with a chunky mash rather than creamy and smooth: it has become my go-to, a happy compromise between my greed and my laziness (I loathe peeling potatoes). I quite enjoy the added rustic texture and flavor that you get from the skins, but obviously, if you prefer your mashed potatoes smooth, then peel them before following the recipe. Once laced with plenty of salted butter and the pops of intensely flavored and scented preserved lemon, it's good either way. Mashed potatoes should be enjoyed piping hot, so either make them and bring them straight to the table, or make them in advance and simply reheat them gently in a saucepan on the stove or microwave (see instructions, above). All of which makes this dish a great thing to drop off, perhaps alongside a chicken pie or a cooked roast chicken (see pages 46 and 43), which can then be enjoyed at room temperature alongside the hot mashed potatoes.

HANDS ON TIME:
15 minutes
HANDS OFF TIME:
10–15 minutes cooking
SERVES 6–8

4lbs potatoes
1 stick salted butter
3 preserved lemons, seeds
 and flesh discarded, skin
 finely chopped
flaky sea salt and freshly
 ground black pepper

Cut the potatoes into rough chunks, 1½–2 inches in size. Toss into a saucepan and cover with cold water and a generous dash of salt. Set over a high heat and bring to a boil. When the water begins to gallop, reduce the heat a little and let simmer for 10–15 minutes, until the potatoes are cooked. You should be able to insert a fork into a potato and feel no resistance.

Drain the potatoes in a colander, then toss them back into the saucepan.

While the potatoes are still hot and steaming, throw in the butter and the chopped preserved lemon skin.

Mash together until you have bashed out the lumps. Season to taste with salt and a little pepper.

Mustardy Potato Salad

🎁 *Tip into an airtight container. It will keep in the fridge for two or three days.*

I love this way of preparing buttery fingerling potatoes, just drenched in a simple mustard dressing and showered in frilly, verdant parsley leaves. It's simplicity itself and gloriously moreish to eat. You can make this in advance and happily serve it at room temperature; in fact, I can't help but feel that the flavors improve and intensify a little once they've had a bit of time to develop. Depending on my mood, sometimes I make this with English mustard, which gives the salad a gloriously intense sunny yellow color, but also a punchy flavor. Other times, when what I crave is something more mellow, I make it with Dijon.

HANDS ON TIME:
15 minutes
HANDS OFF TIME:
15–20 minutes cooking
SERVES 6-8

2¼lbs fingerling potatoes
5 tbsp olive oil
2 heaped tbsp English
    mustard, or Dijon
    mustard (see recipe
    introduction)
2 tbsp white wine vinegar
handful of parsley leaves,
    coarsely chopped
flaky sea salt

Put the potatoes in a large saucepan, cover with cold water, salt generously and set over a medium-high heat. Bring to a boil and, once the water begins to gallop, reduce the heat. Simmer for 15–20 minutes, until the potatoes are cooked through. Cooking time will vary a little depending on the size of the potatoes, but to test if they're done, insert a fork or knife into a potato: it should feel little or no resistance.

Drain the water and toss the potatoes back into the pan. Drizzle over half the olive oil and season with a little salt.

In a small bowl, lightly whisk the mustard and the vinegar together until you have a creamy, bright yellow concoction (if using English mustard; Dijon will be a softer beige). Pour this over the potatoes and toss so they are all covered.

Now, drizzle over the last of the olive oil and toss again. Season with a little more salt if you like. Most especially if using English mustard, the potatoes will taste very peppery at this point: don't panic, the flavor will mellow a little as they cool.

When the potatoes are at room temperature, sprinkle over the parsley and toss together for a final time before serving.

Coffee and Ricotta Cream Roulade

✉ *Drop off in a cake box (I buy these in bulk online) or on a plate covered with reusable food wrap, with instructions to store in the fridge. It will keep for up to two days.*

It's the unadulterated messiness of this, bursting at its seams with cream, that I love so much: sponge as light as air, whipped coffee-scented cream, silky-smooth and sweet but not overly so. I'd eat this for breakfast, or as a dessert, and can think of few things that would cheer me up more than to find one sitting on my doorstep. Add shards of bittersweet chocolate or walnuts (or both) to the cream, if you like.

HANDS ON TIME:
25 minutes

HANDS OFF TIME:
8–10 minutes in the oven;
1 hour cooling;
30 minutes chilling

SERVES 8

FOR THE SPONGE
butter, for the pan
4 eggs
½ cup (100g) superfine
　sugar, plus 2 tbsp
¾ cup (100g) all-purpose
　flour
1 tbsp instant espresso
　powder

FOR THE CREAM
2 cups (500g) ricotta
1½ cups (150g)
　confectioners' sugar
1 tbsp instant espresso
　powder
unsweetened cocoa
　powder, to dust

Heat the oven to 400°F. Butter a jelly roll pan measuring 15 x 10 inches and line with parchment paper.

Whisk the eggs and the ½ cup sugar in a bowl, until it doubles in volume and becomes a pale lemony color. When you lift out the whisk, it should leave a ribbon-like trail behind. Sift in one-third of the flour and fold through, then repeat with the rest of the flour, a little at a time. Lastly fold through the coffee powder.

Pour the batter into the prepared pan and level it out with a spoon, so the entire pan is covered. Don't worry if it doesn't seem enough: it will rise a lot in the oven. Bake for 8–10 minutes, until the cake is just colored and a knife comes out clean when you insert it to the middle.

While the cake is still hot from the oven, sprinkle the 2 tbsp superfine sugar over the top, covering as much of the surface as you can, then lay a sheet of parchment paper over the cake and quickly flip it over. Remove the old parchment paper from underneath and lay over a new, clean sheet. Using the parchment underneath as an aid, roll the cake and leave to cool for 1 hour on a wire rack.

Meanwhile, make the filling: spoon the ricotta into a mixing bowl, sift in the confectioners' sugar and beat with a wooden spoon until smooth. Now add the coffee powder and beat again until well combined and the ricotta is a smooth coffee color. Set the ricotta cream in the fridge to chill, while you wait for the sponge to cool completely.

When the cake roll is cold, gently unroll it. Spread the ricotta cream over the surface, leaving a 1-inch margin round the edge, then re-roll. Refrigerate for 30 minutes – or put in the freezer for 10 minutes – then dust with cocoa powder before serving.

Orange Treacle Tart

Store in a cake box (I buy these in bulk online) with instructions to reheat gently in the oven (or a slice at a time in the microwave). Include a container of ice cream.

There is something innately nostalgic and ever-comforting about the fudgy sweet stickiness of treacle tart. Mine is made with bitter marmalade, which I prefer to golden syrup as I find it less cloying and more layered with flavor. I then top the tart with ruby-stained slices of orange, juices seeping out into the tart and edges gloriously chewy and caramelized. I make this in winter, when intensely red blood oranges are in season, but milder, paler ones do well too; though blood oranges are smaller so you'll need more fruits.

HANDS ON TIME:
25 minutes
HANDS OFF TIME:
1 hour to roast the oranges;
45–50 minutes to bake
the tart
SERVES 6-8

6 blood oranges (or
    4 regular oranges),
    half sliced into
    roughly ⅛-inch rounds,
    half juiced
generous ⅓ cup superfine
    sugar
1 store-bought refrigerated
    pie crust (from a 14.1-oz
    package)
1¾ cups bitter orange
    marmalade
5 cups soft fresh white
    breadcrumbs
lightly whipped cream,
    to serve (optional)

Heat the oven to 350°F.

Arrange the orange slices in a double layer in a shallow baking dish. Pour over the orange juice and sprinkle over ¼ cup sugar, then cover with foil. Roast for 1 hour until the oranges are tender, then set to one side.

Drape the pastry over a 9-inch loose-bottomed tart pan, press it into the pan and prick the bottom with a fork to stop it puffing up too much in the oven. Cover with parchment paper and fill with baking beans. Blind-bake in this manner for 15 minutes, until the pastry looks golden on the edges. Remove the baking beans and parchment and cook for a further 5 minutes, until the pastry feels dry to the touch.

While the crust is baking, warm the marmalade in a medium-sized saucepan over a medium heat, until all melted and syrupy. Take the pan off the heat, add the breadcrumbs and stir together with a wooden spoon until you have a thick, sticky paste.

Spoon the syrupy filling into the tart crust and smooth out with the back of your spoon. Arrange the orange slices over the filling, overlapping and in concentric circles, so the entire surface is covered in a blanket of candied orange. Drizzle the last of the orange juices over the fruit, then set the tart back in the oven and bake for a further 20 minutes.

Take the tart out of the oven, sprinkle with the remaining sugar, then put back in one last time for 5–10 minutes until the oranges are deliciously caramelized. Serve warm, ideally with lightly whipped cream.

Chocolate, Coconut and Cherry Cake

⊞ *Stored in a cake box, this will keep somewhere cool for three days.*

A fudgy, dense chocolate cake – not overly sweet, though the creamy snow-white frosting is deliciously so – peppered with black and inimitably sour cherries. Inspiration for this comes from Cherry Ripe bars, an Aussie staple, sticky coconut dipped in bittersweet chocolate, studded with sour cherries. I remember packing as many bars as I could carry into my knapsack at the end of the holidays in Australia and smuggling them back into Europe to ration and savor over the coming months.

HANDS ON TIME:
25 minutes

HANDS OFF TIME:
60–70 minutes in the oven

SERVES 8–10

FOR THE CAKE
butter, for the pan
2¼ cups (280g) all-
    purpose flour, plus 1 tbsp
3¾ tsp baking powder
1¾ cups (140g)
    unsweetened shredded
    coconut, plus 2 tbsp
¾ cup (70g) unsweetened
    cocoa powder
4 eggs
1½ cups (300g) superfine
    sugar
7 tbsp (100g) vegetable oil
1⅔ cups (400g) coconut-
    flavored yogurt
¾ cup (160g) drained
    amarena cherries
flaky sea salt

FOR THE FROSTING
1¼ cups (300g) cream
    cheese
1½ cups (150g)
    confectioners' sugar
2 tsp cornstarch
½ cup (120g) heavy cream

Heat the oven to 350°F. Butter a 9-inch springform cake pan and line it with parchment paper.

Combine the 2¼ cups flour, baking powder, 1¾ cups coconut and cocoa powder in a mixing bowl. In a second bowl, combine the eggs and sugar and whisk until the mixture has doubled in volume and turned a pale lemony color. Add the oil in a steady trickle, whisking all the while. Now spoon in the yogurt and whisk until smooth. Add the dry ingredients, a spoonful at a time, again whisking all the while.

Spoon the cherries into the mixing bowl you used for the dry ingredients (to save on dishwashing), sprinkle over the 1 tbsp flour and shake them about so the syrupy cherries are all evenly coated. Now fold the cherries into the cake mixture.

Spoon the batter into the prepared pan and bake for 60–70 minutes until the sponge bounces back when you press down on it gently and a knife comes out clean when inserted to the middle: if the cake is browning too much and looks like it might catch, cover it with foil as it bakes.

Let the cake cool in the pan for 10 minutes, then turn it out on to a wire rack and let cool completely before frosting.

Lightly beat the cream cheese, sift in the confectioners' sugar and cornstarch, then beat again until smooth and combined. Pour in the cream and beat until you have smooth white frosting of a spreadable consistency.

Set the cake on a stand or platter, top generously with the creamy frosting, then sprinkle over the 2 tbsp coconut so it looks like it's dusted in snow.

More S'mores Pie

🎁 *Store in a cake box (I buy these in bulk online) with instructions to keep chilled, or else the base has a tendency to crumble. It will keep in the fridge for two or three days.*

As a child I remember eating s'mores – graham cracker sandwiches filled with melting chocolate and charred marshmallow – by the campfire with Wendy. It was Wendy who first taught me about s'mores, just as she taught me about peanut butter and banana sandwiches, apple – crisp and sweet – paired with cheese, how to tie my shoelaces, that you don't have to be family to love each other like family, and how to bake a cake for no other good reason than just for the fun of it. So many of the things that bring me joy in life, I learned from Wendy.

Still now I love s'mores: I look forward to those days when we get the barbecue going in our back garden, so that the boys and I can make them. This pie is a variation on the same theme: a buttery crumbled graham cracker base, chocolate cream filling and clouds of burnished meringue on top which has a fluffy, chewy, marshmallow-like quality about it.

It's a three-part recipe, where you make each of the base, filling and topping separately and then assemble, all of which might seem like a bit of a faff (most especially the meringue topping where you whisk it over boiling water to get that chewy marshmallow texture), but I promise you that each of the steps are intuitively simple and the result is a confection of such utter delight for children and grown-ups alike that it is well worth the effort. If it makes life simpler, you can also make the pie in stages.

And if you don't have a torch lighter, heat the oven to 350°F and put the pie – straight from the fridge – in for 15 minutes, until golden and burnished on top.

Recipe continues overleaf

HANDS ON TIME:
30 minutes
HANDS OFF TIME:
2 hours in the fridge
SERVES 8-10

FOR THE BASE
2 sticks salted butter
1 14-oz box graham
   crackers
⅓ cup superfine sugar

FOR THE FILLING
⅔ cup heavy cream
7oz bittersweet chocolate,
   very finely chopped

FOR THE TOPPING
4 egg whites
1 cup superfine sugar
½ tsp cream of tartar

In a small saucepan, gently melt the butter over a low heat, then take off the heat. Blitz the crackers into crumbs in a food processor, then add the melted butter and sugar and blitz again until all combined. If you don't have a processor, you can just crumble the crackers as finely as possible into the pan of melted butter and stir in the sugar. Press the cracker crumbs into a 9-inch loose-bottomed tart pan, so the base and about ¾ inches up the sides are all covered.

Warm the cream in a small saucepan over a medium-low heat. Just before it comes to a boil (you should see small bubbles forming at the edge of the pan), pour it over the finely chopped chocolate in a heatproof bowl and stir until completely melted. Pour the thick chocolate cream into the tart crust and put in the fridge for 1–2 hours, until it feels set when you touch it.

Lastly make the marshmallow topping: put the egg whites, sugar and cream of tartar in a heatproof bowl and set the bowl over a saucepan of boiling water, taking care not to let the boiling water touch the bowl. Using a hand-held electric mixer, whisk constantly for 4 minutes, until you have a fluffy white mixture and all the sugar is dissolved. To test if the sugar has dissolved, rub a little of the cloudy meringue between your fingers (careful, as it will be hot): you shouldn't feel any sugar granules. Take the bowl off the heat and keep whisking for a further 5 minutes, until very glossy and stiff.

Spoon the marshmallow over the chocolate cream and spread it out with the back of the spoon. If you have a torch lighter, use it to burnish or toast the marshmallow (if you don't, see recipe introduction). Store the pie in the fridge until you're ready to serve it.

Salted Caramel Apple Crumble

✤ *Prepare in a baking dish and cover with foil. Reheat gently in the oven, still covered with foil. It keeps for up to two days. Or freeze before cooking and bake from frozen.*

I can't help but feel that crumble is overrated: I enjoy it, but there are so many other desserts I would gladly choose over it. But this crumble – the fruit layered with pockets of salted caramel and topped with a rubble of almost-caramelized cracker crumbs – I could eat daily. The topping, a fudgy concoction of crumbled graham crackers and lightly browned sugar, comes from Claire Macdonald's *Seasonal Cooking* and tastes like no other: it is incomparable. I give my own recipe for salted caramel to drizzle over the just-softened fruit: it is wonderfully simple. Though if the thought of a second pan to clean feels like a bridge too far (or you're pressed for time), feel free to use store-bought caramel from a tube or jar; you will need about 1½ cups. While it's always an inaccurate science to guesstimate how many more or less hungry people any single dish will serve, I caution that while the dessert doesn't look quite enough for ten, it's rich and a little goes a deliciously long way.

HANDS ON TIME:
20 minutes
HANDS OFF TIME:
20-25 minutes in the oven
SERVES 8-10

2 sticks plus 5 tbsp
    salted butter
1¾ cups light brown sugar
3 tbsp Lyle's golden syrup
⅔ cup sweetened
    condensed milk
3lbs apples, cored (no need
    to peel), chopped into
    small pieces
7 tbsp cold water
13oz graham crackers
    (approximately
    22 sheets)
flaky sea salt

Heat the oven to 350°F.

Start by making the salted caramel: melt 4 tbsp of the butter in a small saucepan over a medium heat. Add 7 tbsp of the sugar, the golden syrup and the condensed milk. Stir constantly with a wooden spoon over the heat until the sauce is thick, smooth and darkened a little, which will take 1-2 minutes: if you taste it, it should feel smooth in your mouth, you shouldn't be able to feel the graininess of the sugar. When you have a caramel, take it off the heat, add a generous pinch of salt and stir in.

Toss the apples into a large, ovenproof roasting pan (mine is about 11 x 7 inches) and add the measured cold water. Simmer over a medium heat for 3-5 minutes, so the apples soften just a little, then drain any excess juices. Drizzle the caramel over the apples and toss the pieces together so the sauce is evenly distributed throughout.

In a second small saucepan, melt the remaining butter. Crumble the crackers into the melted butter and add the last of the sugar. Mash and mix everything together with a wooden spoon, to break up the crackers so you have something that resembles wet sand. Now spoon the crumble over the apple, spreading it out evenly so as to cover the surface.

Set the crumble in the oven to bake for 20-25 minutes until lightly golden on top.

Torta alla Meringata

⊞ Store in a cake box (you can buy these online). This will keep for a day in the fridge, but not for much longer.

I won't lie: this cake can be a bit of a palaver to make and so is perhaps not best suited for those days when you seek instant gratification; instead it's for when you want extravagant, sumptuous sweet folly. The recipe may be a labor of love, but in return for your efforts comes a cloud-like confection of such utter delight that it is undoubtedly more than worth it: so much sweet, vanilla-scented whipped cream layered with thin layers of sponge that it seems almost structurally improbable, but tastes like a bite of heaven, then all enrobed in soft Italian meringue.

Inspiration comes from the *torta alla meringata* that they serve at Harry's Dolci in Venice and which remains one of my all-time favorite desserts (just as it is one of my favorite restaurants). Were I to have the privilege to choose my last supper, it most certainly would feature – in star place – on the menu.

My adaptation here is simplified a little to better fit in with the limitations and practicalities of a home kitchen, but tastes none the less exquisite for it.

This dish contains raw or lightly cooked eggs so may not be suitable for people with a weakened immune system, such as babies and very young children, the pregnant and the elderly.

HANDS ON TIME:
45 minutes
HANDS OFF TIME:
1–1¼ hours in the oven;
35 minutes cooling
SERVES 10–12

FOR THE CAKE
3 sticks (340g) salted
   butter, softened, plus
   more for the pans
5¼ cups (660g) all-
   purpose flour
5 tsp baking powder
3 cups plus 3 tbsp (640g)
   superfine sugar
8 eggs
1⅓ cups (330ml) whole
   milk
3 tsp vanilla extract

FOR THE FILLING
3⅓ cups (800g) heavy
   cream
1 cup (100g) confectioners'
   sugar
3 tsp vanilla extract

FOR THE MERINGUE
6 egg whites
1½ cups (300g) superfine
   sugar
2 tsp vanilla extract

Heat the oven to 350°F. Butter 2 springform 9-inch cake pans and line them with parchment paper.

For the cake, combine the flour and baking powder in a bowl.

In a second bowl, beat the butter until soft and creamy, then add the superfine sugar and beat until fluffy. Beating all the while, add the eggs, one at a time. Lastly, still beating constantly, add the flour in 3 parts, alternating with one-third of the milk and 1 tsp vanilla each time.

Divide the batter between the pans and bake for 1–1¼ hours, until lightly golden on top and, when you insert a toothpick, it comes out dry. Turn the cakes out of the pans and let cool completely on a wire rack.

To make the filling: whip the cream until stiff peaks form. Sift in the confectioners' sugar and add the vanilla, then whip again until combined. Take care not to over-whip: you want the cream to be firm, but not clumpy.

Once the cakes have cooled completely, use a bread knife to cut across each to make 2 halves, as you will have 4 layers.

Set the first layer on a stand or serving dish, then spoon over one-third of the cream and spread it out evenly, leaving a margin of about ¾ inch round the edge. Sandwich with a second layer of cake and repeat until you have a towering cake of sponge and what looks like too much whipped cream. Use a knife or angled spatula to smooth out any excess cream at the edges: you ideally want smooth edges all round, rather than cream spilling out in blobs.

Now for the meringue. In a spotlessly clean mixing bowl, whisk the egg whites until they become frothy, then add the sugar, 1 heaping spoonful at a time, until you have a stiff, glossy meringue. Lastly, whisk in the vanilla.

Spoon the soft meringue over the towering cake and use the back of the spoon to smooth it all over in swirls, so every last bit of the surface is covered in swirly peaks.

Use a torch lighter to burnish the meringue all over so it's exquisitely chewy on the outside.

Decadently Dark No-Churn Chocolate Ice Cream

Nothing heals a broken heart or a bruised soul like chocolate ice cream. And this is perhaps the most outrageously chocolatey of all ice creams: like eating iced chocolate mousse by the spoonful, it's rich and devilishly dark. The recipe below is adapted from Cenk Sönmezsoy's recipe for 'The Best Chocolate Ice Cream You'll Ever Have' which I stumbled upon many years ago on Joanna Goddard's blog, *Cup of Jo*. I've been making it on repeat – and prescribing it to friends and loved ones alike with quasi-evangelical fervor – ever since. The method is no-churn, so no need for an ice cream maker, which suits me, my lazy disposition and kitchen gadgetry phobia down to a tee; as does the fact that it's delightfully simple to make. My only caveat is that, like all no-churn ice creams, the texture is ice-block solid when served straight from the freezer, so try if you can to let the container rest on the kitchen counter for 10–15 minutes before serving into bowls or cones. And always make more than you think you'll need: because trust me when I say that you'll eat it.

HANDS ON TIME:
15 minutes
HANDS OFF TIME:
6 hours in the freezer
MAKES about 1 quart

9oz bittersweet chocolate, finely chopped
14-oz can of sweetened condensed milk
scant ½ cup unsweetened cocoa powder, sifted
½ tsp instant espresso powder
1 tsp vanilla extract
1⅔ cups heavy cream
flaky sea salt

Melt two-thirds of the chocolate in a heatproof bowl over a saucepan of barely simmering water, making sure the bowl does not touch the water. Meanwhile, chop the remaining chocolate into chunks and set aside.

Once the chocolate has melted, take the bowl off the heat and add the condensed milk, cocoa powder, espresso powder and vanilla extract, with a large pinch of salt.

In a second bowl, whip the cream until stiff peaks form, taking care not to over-whip it: you want a texture that is luscious and firm, a bit like thick yogurt rather than like mascarpone.

Gently fold the whipped cream into the chocolate mixture. Finally, fold in the remaining chocolate chunks.

Pour the mixture into a 5-cup container and freeze for at least 6 hours.

Pistachio and Fig Queen of Puddings

This tastes like a cloud, a warm cloud: the meringue soft, puffy and airy and the eggy, custardy pudding underneath it every bit as delectable and soothing. Queen of Puddings is one of those nostalgic dishes I didn't actually grow up with, but because it featured so temptingly in so many of the storybooks of my childhood, I somehow feel as though I did. I like to add a handful of chopped pistachios to the base, which is by no means traditional, but I find gives not just flavor but also a little more texture. You could of course make this with almonds instead of pistachios if you prefer, or leave the nuts out completely. And if you can't find fig preserves, then raspberry or strawberry – or even a nice bitter marmalade – will do every bit as well.

HANDS ON TIME:
20 minutes
HANDS OFF TIME:
20 minutes resting;
40–50 minutes in the oven
SERVES 4-6

2½ cups whole milk
2 cups coarse fresh white
  breadcrumbs
¾ cup superfine sugar
½ cup shelled pistachios,
  finely chopped
1 tbsp salted butter
4 eggs, separated
¾ cup fig preserves
chilled cream, to serve

Bring the milk to just before a boil in a small, heavy-based saucepan over a medium heat. When tiny bubbles begin to form at the edge of the pan, take the milk off the heat and tip in the breadcrumbs, 2 tbsp of the sugar and all the pistachio nuts and butter. Set to one side and leave for 20 minutes or so to let the breadcrumbs swell.

Heat the oven to 350°F.

Lightly beat the egg yolks and add them to the cooled breadcrumb mixture, then pour it all into a 10-inch pie dish. Use the back of a spoon to spread it out evenly over the bottom of the dish.

Bake in the center of the oven for 30–35 minutes, until set.

In a small saucepan, gently heat the fig preserves to melt. When the pudding is ready, take it out of the oven and spread the preserves over the top, taking care to distribute it evenly across the surface.

In a clean mixing bowl, use a hand-held electric mixer to beat the egg whites until they begin to stiffen. Spoon by spoon, add the remaining sugar, whisking all the while. Either pipe or spoon the meringue over the preserves, taking care that the meringue covers the edge of the dish as well as its contents and that there are no gaps.

Bake in the oven for a further 10–15 minutes, until the meringue topping is a light golden brown.

Serve warm, with chilled cream.

Salted Chocolate Chip Cookies

⊞ Store in an airtight container, a cookie jar, cake box, or simply wrap up in a reusable food wrap bundle. The baked cookies will keep happily somewhere cool for up to four days. Alternatively, drop off a batch of raw cookie dough (either cookie-sized dough balls stored in a resealable bag, or just a lump of dough wrapped in parchment paper), along with baking instructions. The dough will keep in the fridge for up to three days, and it also freezes beautifully, for cookies on demand. I also have a soft spot for eating it raw, but perhaps that's just me...

It comes in peaks and troughs, the longing for really good cookies. My cravings intensify when life feels more challenging: when I'm down, cookies – home-baked and still warm from the oven – are what I want to eat.

These cookies are big: they're chewy in the middle, almost to the point of being soft raw dough at the very center, which is how I like them best, because the one thing I love to eat more than cookies is cookie dough. However, if you prefer them crumbly rather than chewy, simply leave them to bake in the oven for a couple of minutes longer.

I use shards of bittersweet or milk chocolate (or both) and the very best kind I can lay my hands on, rather than sweeter but somehow slightly too processed-tasting chocolate chips, along with a generous dash of flaky sea salt both in the dough and sprinkled saucily on top of each round: for me, this is what makes the cookies so very irresistible and somehow like a 'grown-up' treat rather than childish fare. And, like all cookies, these are especially, soul-soothingly good when eaten still warm.

HANDS ON TIME:
10 minutes
HANDS OFF TIME:
5–10 minutes chilling;
6–10 minutes in the oven;
MAKES 16 large cookies

3¼ cups (400g) all-
    purpose flour
4 tsp baking powder
6oz (150g) bittersweet or
    milk chocolate, chopped
1 stick plus 3 tbsp (170g)
    salted butter
¾ cup (150g) dark brown
    sugar
½ cup (100g) superfine
    sugar
2 eggs
flaky sea salt

In a small mixing bowl, whisk together the flour and baking powder, then mix in the chocolate chunks along with 1 tsp salt.

Melt the butter in a small saucepan over a low heat.

Combine the liquid butter and both kinds of sugar together in a large mixing bowl and beat with a hand-held electric mixer until you have a smooth paste.

Lightly beat the eggs with a fork in a small bowl or cup. Once the butter has cooled enough not to cook the eggs (test the temperature by putting your finger in), beat in the eggs until you have something that resembles a dark, runny caramel. Add the dry ingredients to the wet and give everything a good stir with a wooden spoon to combine. Set in the fridge for 5–10 minutes to firm the dough up a little.

Heat the oven to 350°F. Line 2 baking sheets with parchment paper.

Scoop 1 heaping tbsp of the cookie dough and roll into a ball, roughly the size of a golf ball. Set the balls of dough on the lined baking sheets, leaving a lot of space between each as they will spread in the oven. Press down on each ball to flatten it a little, then sprinkle a pinch of flaky salt over each little mound.

Set in the oven and bake for 6–7 minutes for cookies that are very doughy in the middle, or 8–10 minutes for cookies that are a little firmer.

Take the cookies out of the oven and, while they're still warm (and soft to touch), shape each one by putting a wide-rimmed glass over it and spinning it round in a clockwise motion: you don't want to trim away the dough here, just to bounce the warm cookies gently off the rim of the glass to shape them and give you perfectly round cookies.

Let cool on the baking sheet for 10–15 minutes (if you can!) before eating.

SEDUCE

Some thoughts on romance, and recipes to (perhaps)
make someone fall in love with you

When I have a wobble, I let my mind wander back to the little house on the cobbled Oxford back street, affectionately known as 'pink house' because its walls are painted a saccharine shade of English rose pink. I settle there, in the kitchen down in the basement with not much by way of natural light, fairly rudimentary fittings and decor that you might charitably call dated. Because there, in that unassuming little kitchen that smells like buttery crêpe batter, like sizzling sausages and fried cheap white bread, is where I fell in love with the man who is now my husband.

Anthony and I were both college freshers when we met: he was studying math, while my subject was classics. Our paths probably shouldn't have crossed, except we both found ourselves in the same section of the library one day, and then by chance later that same day both happened to be sitting in the same corner of the college bar. Not long after, he made me crêpes on the little electric stove in the pink house.

I remember being very impressed by the way he seemed to know what he was doing, the deftness with which he whisked the batter and flipped the crêpes, all of which seemed like a kind of alchemy to me, back in the days when I didn't think I knew how to cook. The crêpes were good, really good. Still now, some twenty-odd years on, crêpes drenched in sharp lemon juice and sugar are my happy place. And still now, I love it when Anthony makes them for me... which occasionally he will do for my birthday, or on Mother's Day, or just because.

Perhaps it's because we're both greedy that our relationship cemented itself over food, or perhaps it's because we met when we were both escaping the comforts of our childhood homes and seeking new homes to grow into. I found home in him, and it looked like crêpes.

Food, as we all know, can be the most eloquent way to express love. But it is a very effective way to invite love, too, and what follows in this chapter is food to seduce, to butter someone up, to make them believe they can't live without you. That's something you always need a recipe for.

Cooking for someone you don't yet know so well and who you think you might want to get to know better can feel daunting, but on a practical level, at least, it's much easier than cooking for a crowd, because the math works in your favor.

The problems that unexpectedly crop up when you're catering on a larger scale – such as when the frying pan isn't quite big enough to sauté all your ingredients (so you end up crowding, and ruining, them) or the oven won't quite fit everything you need to cook inside (so all your timings go pear-shaped) – don't happen when there are just two of you.

Nonetheless, some pitfalls remain, so here are my thoughts on what you need to do to set yourself up for success. Choose dishes you can share: plates of sumptuous food in the middle of the table for you both to dig into. This looks generous and beautiful and is also far less of a performance than plating everything up individually.

Avoid too much garlic (for obvious reasons). Keep the menu light: no one feels sexy on heavy, greasy food (although I refer you back to the aforementioned fried-bread-in-the-pink-house-on-the-cobbled-street-in-Oxford as evidence that there are happy exceptions to all rules).

Ask your date in advance if there's anything they can't or don't like to eat before you plan the menu, so as to avoid any awkwardness when you sit down at the table (such as the time I spent an afternoon preparing a sausage cassoulet for the man who turned out to be a strict vegetarian).

Above all, keep the cooking really simple and resist the overwhelming temptation to cook-to-impress. Instead, channel effortless seduction: either go with recipes that you know so well that you could make them in your sleep, or try them out ahead of your date. (This is probably the only instance in which I would recommend doing so – I tend to think life's too short to 'practice-cook' anything – but needs sometimes must.)

I'm not usually a big fan of appetizers, as anyone who has ever been for dinner at my place will tell you: I don't like the extra fuss, the hassle of clearing away the plates so soon after sitting down to eat, the dishwashing that an extra course entails. But on date nights, I do think there's something to be said for drawing the meal out over three courses, and many of the recipes here – such as the pasta dishes, the cheese soufflé and the scallops laced with breadcrumbs and melted butter – work equally well as appetizers or entrées. And I always make dessert, because there's nothing better than ending the evening on a sweet note, most especially if it's something you can share,

such as a bowl of tiramisù or a cup of creamy rhubarb-pink syllabub, spoons clinking together flirtatiously. But maybe keep the dessert hidden away in the fridge. That way, if the date isn't quite what you hoped it would be, you can draw the evening to an elegant-but-firm close after the entrée and indulge in (all) the dessert once they've gone.

It can be a nice ice-breaker to share some of the cooking, just the very easiest bits, such as asking your date to mix the cocktails or toss a salad, stir a pot or keep an eye on a pan. Asking for help in the kitchen gives you something to talk about if conversation flows awkwardly to begin with, and most importantly it will instantly make your date feel at home.

Another tip: have something to snack on at the ready, such as potato chips, big fat salty olives, slices of salami, nuts, a hunk of cheese with a small dish of honey – I especially love truffle-infused honey – for dipping, radishes with butter and salt. Lay them all out in the kitchen or living room (or wherever you're going to be) ready for you both to help yourselves. This is strategically important because, firstly, it will help soak up any alcohol that you may or may not be consuming, and secondly, it means that the pressure to get the timings right for dinner doesn't feel quite so acute.

Before anyone arrives, you want to set the scene. Lay the table: it doesn't need to be a formal set-up, in fact it shouldn't be. But there's something very welcoming about arriving at someone's home and feeling that they are expecting you. If you can, dim the lights and light candles; just a few shimmering on the mantel and in the corner here and there, to soften the atmosphere. (Not so much that it feels like you're trying to force romance, because of course there's nothing so unromantic as forced romance.) You want small touches here and there that hint at domestic bliss, even just the illusion of it: a pitcher of flowers on the sideboard, a big bowl of lemons on the table, the scent of something baking in the oven. My go-to for this is the rhubarb and Cheddar tart in this chapter, which smells like happiness in that way that only melted cheese and buttery pastry can.

EPILOGUE

... and a few thoughts on cooking for marriage, some twenty-odd years later

At a dinner party not so long ago, I was talking to another guest, an older woman with long-grown-up children. I was telling her about my idea for this book, and she asked if I might also include in this chapter a recipe for happy marriage?

It's true that cooking for the person you love some twenty years into a relationship is a different proposition from the kind of date-night cooking I talk about here. There's certainly no creating the illusion of domestic bliss, because you already experience domesticity together, blissful or otherwise. To use the Ancient Greek vocabulary, *Eros* (lust) has long morphed into *Pragma* (family love), or something like it. The challenge within a marriage is more about finding time for seduction, remembering that a romantic meal together is still something special to share, even if you've been lucky enough to dine together every night for the best part of a lifetime, and may, by this point, find yourselves taking it somewhat for granted.

Some people have songs that become 'their song', but (perhaps because I'm the world's least musical person) Anthony and I have 'our recipes' instead. There's his crêpes, of course, then there's my tiramisù, the first thing I ever cooked for him and which I still wheel out for special occasions. We've acquired more dishes along the way, too, such as steak the way Anthony does it (on the barbecue, cooked in the embers), and pavlova the way we both like it (chewy in the middle, with lots of cream and no passionfruit). So, the recipes here are intended to seduce, but my hope is that they'll also be there for you to enjoy with that same person for years to come.

And as for what makes a good, solid marriage? If only I had the recipe for that one.

A Very Sexy Cocktail

This is an adaptation of Amber Guinness's 'Pink Wink' cocktail from her beautiful book *A House Party in Tuscany*. It's the pinkness of it, that blushing red, as much as the 'wink' that I love and that somehow seems so appropriate for date nights. The pomegranate juice gives a deep color alongside a rich flavor. It's a very sexy cocktail with just the right amount of bitter and just the right amount of subtle sweetness.

HANDS ON TIME:

5 minutes

MAKES 4

2 cups prosecco

2¾ cups pure pomegranate
   juice

3 tbsp Campari

Pour all the ingredients into a pitcher, mix with a cocktail spoon and chill until you're ready to drink it.

Pour over ice to serve.

Bryony's Clear Bloody Mary

This is an adaptation of Bryony's recipe for a Bloody Mary. It's like magic: the tomatoes start red and, by the time you've finished with them, you have a clear, almost peachy pink, flavorsome juice to mix with ice-cold vodka. Season and dress, as you would a Bloody Mary, with celery, Tabasco and the like. The one non-negotiable component is lots of ice. Because there is some degree of forethought involved in the making of the juice, I've allowed enough in the recipe below for four cocktails (enough for two each): I find it's best to prepare more in advance and keep it in the fridge, then you can mix the cocktails as you like and as the mood suits you. I also find that this recipe is especially perfect for the morning after, as you can let the tomato juices strain overnight: it's one of those cocktails that is every bit as good with breakfast or brunch as it is before dinner.

HANDS ON TIME:
10 minutes
HANDS OFF TIME:
overnight, to strain
the tomatoes
MAKES 4 strong cocktails

FOR THE TOMATO JUICE
(MAKES GENEROUS
1¾ CUPS)
1¾lbs tomatoes, chopped
½ red onion, chopped
6 celery stalks, chopped
flaky sea salt

FOR THE COCKTAILS
vodka
ice
Tabasco sauce, or other
    hot sauce
celery stalks (optional)
freshly ground
    black pepper

Combine the tomatoes, onion and celery together in a blender with a generous pinch of salt and blitz until smooth. Pour the puréed tomato mixture into a cheesecloth-lined strainer or colander, set over a bowl and leave in the fridge to strain overnight.

In the morning, discard the pulp in the strainer. The clear tomato-y tasting liquid in the bowl is your cocktail base.

To make one glass, in a cocktail shaker, shake 3 tbsp vodka and ½ cup clear tomato juice with ice. Add a couple of turns of freshly ground black pepper and 1–2 dashes of Tabasco, to taste. Then shake the cocktail again and strain into a glass over fresh ice. Add a celery stalk, if you like, and serve.

Fusilli with Lardo, Almonds and Honey

Pasta is a dish that works magnificently well for two, and indeed any of the pasta recipes in this book can be scaled down (or up) and would make for excellent date-night food. This recipe – corkscrew-shaped fusilli drizzled in sizzling melted lardo and runny honey, then doused in grated cheese and tossed with toasted golden sliced almonds – has that same pleasingly seductive quality as toast smeared in a thick coating of salty butter and a drizzle of sugary-sweet honey. Don't be put off by the fact that lardo sounds deceptively similar to lard, as the two are very different beasts: lardo is the fat from the upper side of pork, cured in salt with rosemary, black pepper and a variety of other aromatic spices. Some supermarkets will sell it at their butchery or deli counters, but otherwise you can buy lardo, either thinly sliced or, as you want it here, chopped into thick chunks, in many Italian delicatessens. If, however, you can't get hold of it, or you would like to make a lighter, vegetarian version of this pasta, then feel free to substitute with melted salted butter instead, and add a generous dash of flaky salt to balance out the heady sweetness of the honey.

HANDS ON TIME:
20 minutes
SERVES 2

8oz fusilli
3 heaping tbsp sliced
  almonds
½ cup diced lardo
  (½-inch chunks)
2 tbsp olive oil
3 tbsp grated Parmesan
  cheese, or pecorino
  cheese
1 tbsp runny honey
flaky sea salt and freshly
  ground black pepper

Bring a large saucepan of generously salted water to a boil. When the water begins to gallop, add the pasta and cook *al dente*, following the package instructions.

Set a non-stick frying pan over a medium heat and toast the sliced almonds for 1–2 minutes until golden in color, then set to one side.

In a large frying pan (large enough to hold the cooked pasta) set over a medium-low heat, gently fry the lardo for 12–15 minutes until the chunks turn crisp and begin to drip fat. Take off the heat. Leave the fat in the pan but take the pieces out and set to one side.

When the pasta is done, scoop a scant ½ cup of the cooking water out and reserve, then drain the pasta in a colander.

Toss the cooked fusilli in the frying pan with the melted lardo, then add the reserved cooking water and drizzle with the olive oil. Fry for a couple of minutes over a high heat, then take the pan off the heat.

Add the Parmesan and toss for a moment or so. Drizzle over the honey, then top with the crisp lardo pieces, toasted almonds and a good grinding of black pepper. Serve immediately.

Spaghetti with Chiles and Hazelnut

It's the fiery heat from the red pepper flakes – warming without being overtly spicy – that makes this dish so very appropriate for a hot-date dinner. Of course, you can add chiles to most pasta dishes, but there is something about the heat of the fire-hot flakes here with buttery, lightly toasted hazelnuts that I especially enjoy. I also relish the utter simplicity of this recipe: you can throw it together in moments with ingredients that you keep in your cabinets, all of which makes it more than ideal for last-minute plans.

HANDS ON TIME:
15 minutes
SERVES 2

8oz spaghetti
¼ cup olive oil
1 garlic clove, peeled
½ tsp crushed red pepper
   flakes
½ cup skinned hazelnuts,
   finely chopped
flaky sea salt

Bring a medium saucepan of generously salted water to a boil. When the water starts to gallop, add the pasta and cook *al dente*, following the package instructions.

Meanwhile, in a medium frying pan, heat the oil, whole garlic clove and red pepper flakes over a medium heat for a few seconds, then add roughly three-quarters of the hazelnuts and fry gently for 1–2 minutes, until they begin to turn golden brown.

Scoop a ladleful of the pasta cooking water out of its saucepan and add it to the pan with the nuts, then let the nuts simmer for 2–3 minutes until most of the liquid has evaporated.

When the pasta is cooked, drain in a colander and toss into the frying pan. Toss together over a gentle heat, so that all the strands of pasta are coated in sauce. Remove and discard the garlic, then sprinkle the last of hazelnuts over the pasta before serving while still piping hot.

Rhubarb and Cheddar Tart

🎁 *This travels most easily on the pan it was baked on, just covered with reusable food wrap. It keeps for up to two days in the fridge, just warm gently in the oven to serve.*

It's the Valentine's sugar-pink of the rhubarb, blushing under a blanket of melted Cheddar, that makes this feel like romantic food for me; though it's the flavor – rhubarb's intense earthy sourness counterbalanced by rich buttery pastry and melting cheese – that makes me long to eat it. As much as you might associate rhubarb with desserts and nursery fare, don't be fooled: this is very much a savory business and also very much a 'grown-up' dish. I'll be honest: the portions here are more than generous for two, but to make half a tart seems mean, and this is one of those dishes that everyone always eats more of than seems sensible, so I prefer to err on the side of plenty. And while it really does taste its very best warm straight from the oven, the cheese melting in your mouth, I nonetheless always look forward to leftovers. To go with it, you only need a salad: I can't resist pairing this with a similarly pastel-hued salad of blush-pink radicchio rosa or dark red bitter endive. Too much? Or just enough? One warning: this works best with long, thin, furiously pink rhubarb stems rather than the fatter ones, which take longer to cook and can taste a little too sharp.

HANDS ON TIME:
10 minutes

HANDS OFF TIME:
25–30 minutes in the oven;
10 minutes cooling

SERVES 4, or **2** with plenty
of leftovers

1 sheet of puff pastry,
    thawed if frozen
1 egg, lightly beaten
heaping ¾ cup mascarpone
2 tbsp grated Parmesan
    cheese
4–6 thin stalks of bright
    pink rhubarb (about
    10oz)
1 tbsp granulated sugar
1 cup grated Cheddar
    cheese
a few sprigs of thyme
flaky sea salt and freshly
    ground black pepper

Heat the oven to 400°F. Line a baking sheet with parchment paper and unroll the sheet of pastry on to the pan. Use a sharp knife to score a 1-inch border around the edge, then prick all over the center part with a fork.

Brush the pastry edge with the egg, then line with parchment paper and baking beans. Blind-bake in the oven for 10 minutes, until dry to the touch and lightly golden at the edges. Take out of the oven and leave to cool for 10 minutes or so.

In a small bowl, combine the mascarpone with the Parmesan and season generously with salt and pepper. Spoon the mascarpone over the middle of the tart and spread it out as evenly as you can. If the pastry is puffed up in the middle, don't worry, just press it down gently with your hands and spoon the mascarpone on top. Cut the rhubarb into long-ish pieces, roughly 6 inches long, and arrange them snugly, side by side like soldiers, over the mascarpone. Sprinkle the sugar over the rhubarb, then top with the grated Cheddar. Lastly scatter over a few thyme leaves.

Set in the oven to bake for 15–20 minutes, until the cheese is melted and the rhubarb is tender. Serve warm.

Scallops with Buttery Brandy Gratin

Not the kind of dish that I would ever cook for a crowd, but this feels like a very special treat for two, served on the scallops' peacock tail-shaped shells, rolled in golden breadcrumbs and swimming in little pools of melted butter and warming brandy. Ask the fishmonger to clean the scallops and their shells for you; then, once you've used them, you can wash the shells and keep them to use again in the future. And for added ease – and because these really must be eaten straight from the oven while still bubbling and warm – I like to prepare the scallops in advance: tuck them into their shells cocooned under their blankets of breadcrumbs and chopped parsley and store in the fridge, then, when you're ready to eat, just put them in the oven.

HANDS ON TIME:
10 minutes
HANDS OFF TIME:
10 minutes in the oven
SERVES 2

3 tbsp salted butter

1 garlic clove, peeled

leaves from a small bunch
of parsley, chopped

1 cup coarse fresh white
breadcrumbs

pinch of freshly grated
nutmeg

2 tbsp brandy, plus more
if needed

4 sea scallops, cleaned,
with their half-shells

flaky sea salt and freshly
ground black pepper

Heat the oven to 425°F.

In a small frying pan, melt the butter and brown the garlic clove for 3–5 minutes over a gentle heat. Toss in the parsley, then take the pan off the heat and give everything a good stir.

Add the breadcrumbs, little by little, stirring well so all the crumbs are coated in butter. Now add the nutmeg, stir again to combine and season with salt and pepper to taste. Finally add the brandy and stir through: you should have a mixture that feels like damp sand. If it feels too dry, then add a dash more brandy. Remove the garlic clove.

Arrange the scallop shells on a baking sheet (I like to lay each on a little bed of scrunched-up foil to stop it rolling around on the pan), then nestle a single scallop inside each shell and cover under a blanket of gratin. Use your fingers to press down the gratin evenly so that the entire scallop is hidden under the buttery breadcrumbs.

Set the pan in the oven and bake for 10 minutes.

Roasted Dorade with Fennel and Tomatoes

This is a delightfully simple dish to prepare: the lion's share of the effort lies in sourcing good, fresh dorade and asking your fishmonger to clean and gut it for you. For the rest, it's largely a matter of assembling the ingredients in a roasting pan and putting it in the oven. If you wanted, for ease, you could prepare the dish largely in advance with the tomatoes and lightly blanched sweet fennel, then let everything sit in the pan in the fridge until you're ready to roast it (if you do, you may want to increase the cooking time by just a smidgen, or bring the fish to room temperature before cooking it).

HANDS ON TIME:
10 minutes
HANDS OFF TIME:
20-25 minutes in the oven
SERVES 2

1 small fennel bulb, with lots of its fennel herb fronds, if possible
2 small whole dorade, gutted and cleaned
small bunch of thyme
5 tbsp olive oil
1⅓ cups cherry or grape tomatoes, halved
1 tbsp capers
flaky sea salt and freshly ground black pepper

Heat the oven to 350°F.

Bring a small saucepan of generously salted water to a boil. Chop the fennel into quarters. When the water begins to gallop, throw the fennel in and cook for 3 minutes, then drain and slice the fennel.

Meanwhile, wash the fish under cold running water to get rid of any excess blood, then pat dry with paper towels. Stuff each dorade with some thyme, saving a little to scatter in the pan later.

Drizzle 2–3 tbsp olive oil over a roasting pan and put the fish on it, side by side. Scatter the tomatoes, capers and sliced fennel around the fish, with all the fennel herb that came with it. Toss in a couple of thyme sprigs, drizzle over the last of the olive oil and season generously with salt and pepper.

Roast in the oven for 20-25 minutes, until the fish flesh is opaque.

Cheese and Marmite Soufflé

Soufflé used to scare me. And then one of my mother's friends, Lucy, was telling how – for the first year of her marriage – she cooked cheese soufflé for dinner every night for her and her husband, as she couldn't cook, but could just about rustle together eggs and cheese. I thought I would give it a try. And now, I urge you to do the same. Like much in life, it turns out that soufflés are just a matter of timing: bake this for exactly 25 minutes and do not open the oven a moment sooner. Your reward is a cloud-like concoction, pudding-like in the middle and golden-crisp at the edge. If you prefer a soufflé that is firmer all the way through, you should bake it for 30 minutes, but categorically no longer. One last suggestion: to minimize fuss, make the cheese sauce and prepare the dish in advance. Then, once your guest arrives and no further delays are guaranteed, whisk the egg whites, fold them into the sauce and bake.

HANDS ON TIME:
20 minutes
HANDS OFF TIME:
25–30 minutes in the oven
SERVES 2

3 tbsp salted butter, plus
    more for the dish
1 heaping tbsp fresh white
    breadcrumbs
2 tsp Marmite
⅓ cup all-purpose flour
¾ cup plus 1 tbsp whole
    milk
3 eggs
heaping ¾ cup grated sharp
    Cheddar cheese
flaky sea salt and freshly
    ground black pepper

Heat the oven to 400°F and put a baking sheet on the middle shelf. Generously butter a 6-inch soufflé dish, sprinkle in the crumbs and rotate, so the sides and base are coated. Tip out the excess crumbs.

In a small saucepan, melt the butter over a medium heat. Add the Marmite and stir until melted into the butter, then pour in the flour and stir vigorously until you have a thick, smooth paste. Take off the heat and gradually pour in the milk, little by little, stirring constantly: take care to mix in each splash, so you have a smooth sauce, before you add more. Return to the heat and stir until the sauce becomes very thick. This should take 3–5 minutes. Transfer the mixture to a mixing bowl and let cool.

Separate the eggs and set the whites in a clean mixing bowl. Stir the yolks into the Marmite mixture. Stir in the cheese and season to taste. At this point, you can set the sauce to one side and come back to it later, if you like.

Use a hand-held electric mixer to beat the egg whites until stiff peaks form; then gently stir the whites into the cheese sauce, drawing a figure of 8 with your wooden spoon, and trying to keep as much air in there as you can.

Spoon the mixture into the prepared dish. Put on the baking sheet and bake for 25–30 minutes, until the top is golden and risen and has a slight wobble to it. Take care not to open the oven door before the first 25 minutes of cooking time, or the soufflé will collapse.

Serve immediately while still piping hot and slightly runny in the center.

Pork Tenderloin with Peaches and Fennel

The idea for this particular pairing comes from my friend Bryony: the peaches – roasted just enough to release their sweet, ambrosial juices but still firmly holding their shape – work a treat with the tender, rich meat. It's a very good match indeed, although when peaches are out of season I also happily make this with plums (using the same method as below).

This is one of those dishes that need delightfully little to go with it, perhaps a crisp green salad, or thinly sliced fennel topped with a drizzle of olive oil and a few shavings of Parmesan or pecorino. A few potatoes (baked, roasted or just boiled and dressed with olive oil, salt and parsley), if you like, but they are by no means necessary and you certainly wouldn't want anything more. And if you want to stretch the meal out a little, you might want to start with some sexy scallops, served on their pretty shells and smothered in buttery gratin (see page 100).

HANDS ON TIME:
20 minutes
HANDS OFF TIME:
1 hour, or up to overnight, to marinate; 15–20 minutes in the oven
SERVES 2

2 tbsp honey
2 tsp Dijon mustard
3 tbsp olive oil
10oz pork tenderloin
2 tsp fennel seeds, crushed
2 peaches, halved
flaky sea salt

Combine the honey, mustard and 1 tbsp olive oil together in a small bowl and whisk together with a fork. Spoon the honey mixture over the tenderloin and rub it all over. Rub in the fennel seeds and a dash of salt. Wrap and leave to marinate in the fridge for at least an hour, or overnight if you can.

Heat the oven to 400°F.

Heat the remaining 2 tbsp olive oil in a large frying pan with an ovenproof handle over a high heat. Sear the pork on all sides until golden brown, add the peaches to the pan, then set in the oven for 15–20 minutes until a meat thermometer registers at 145–150°F.

Let rest for 5–10 minutes, then slice the tenderloin and serve with the peaches.

Buttery Mackerel with Roasted Rhubarb

I adore this pairing: the tender rhubarb, sherbet-sharp, is sweet relief from the richness of the mackerel. The hot pink stems, cooked just long enough to melt in your mouth but still holding their shape, cut through the oiliness of the fish and bring out the intensity of its distinctive flavor. And because I typically make this with pre-cooked smoked mackerel fillets, the kind that come vacuum-packed and that you can buy readily in British supermarkets, I find it's an especially low-maintenance way to cook and serve fish that still feels quite special. If you can't find smoked mackerel fillets, a nice alternative is fresh, or frozen and thawed, rainbow trout fillets, though you will need to adjust the cooking time. You could add a few potatoes on the side, if you like, perhaps fingerling potatoes boiled or steamed and then dressed with olive oil, a squeeze of lemon and a shower of green parsley, or drenched in mustardy dressing (see page 56); either cook in the quantities prescribed there and save leftovers for coming days, or halve the recipe to make enough just for two.

HANDS ON TIME:
5 minutes
HANDS OFF TIME:
10–15 minutes in the oven
SERVES 2

2–3 thin stalks rhubarb
   (about 6oz)
2 tbsp granulated sugar
small bunch of thyme
2 smoked mackerel fillets
1 tbsp butter
juice of ½ lemon

Heat the oven to 400°F.

Cut the rhubarb into 4-inch pieces and arrange the fuchsia-pink stems in a roasting pan. Sprinkle over the sugar and some of the thyme, then cover the pan with foil and set in the oven to bake until the rhubarb is just tender enough to be easily pierced with the tip of a knife, but is still holding its shape nicely. For skinny stems this should take 6–7 minutes; for slightly thicker stalks you'll need more like 10–15 minutes.

Meanwhile, put each mackerel fillet on a large square of foil and top each with half the butter, the last of the thyme and a squeeze of lemon juice. Fold the foil together at the top, crimping around the edges to seal the parcels.

Put on a baking sheet, and cook for 10 minutes, until the butter has melted completely into the fish and the fillets are warmed through. Remove from the oven and transfer the fish to plates. Serve together with the rhubarb and its hot, pink juices.

Roast Duck Legs with Winter Citrus

I love duck cooked this way: the skin salty-crisp like charred paper and the meat mouth-meltingly tender. The potatoes and the orange, sliced thin, cook in the same pan as the duck and infuse with the deeply flavorsome fat from the legs as they roast, intermingling with the sweet juices from the fruit. My preference is to arrange the slices of orange under the meat, as far as possible, which means that they soften and tenderize rather than crisp and turn bitter as they cook in the oven. It's one of those delightful one-pan dishes that constitutes a complete meal in itself, though I often serve it with a bitter leaf salad on the side: just crisp, fresh leaves (ruby-red endive or blush-pink radicchio) dressed with a little olive oil, a squeeze of lemon juice and a generous sprinkling of flaky salt.

HANDS ON TIME:
20 minutes

HANDS OFF TIME:
1¼ hours in the oven;
10 minutes resting

SERVES 2

2 duck legs
2 large potatoes (total
    weight 10–12oz)
1 large orange
small bunch of thyme
flaky sea salt and freshly
    ground black pepper

Heat the oven to 375°F.

Fry the duck legs, skin side down, in a large frying pan (ideally one with a heatproof handle) for 3–5 minutes, until the skin is browned all over. Take the pan off the heat, lift the duck legs on to a plate and set to one side.

Thinly slice the potatoes and the orange into rounds, roughly ¼ inch thick. Arrange most of the slices of orange in the center of the same pan, and lay the duck on top of these, skin-side up. Arrange the potatoes overlapping in a single layer all around the duck and oranges, with the remaining slices of orange peeking out here and there.

Season everything liberally with salt and pepper, sprinkling over a few thyme sprigs. Set in the oven and roast for 1¼ hours, or until both the duck legs and the potatoes are golden and exquisitely crisp.

Rest for 10 minutes before serving.

Orange, Beet and Feta Salad

When we're knee-deep in winter, when the days are short and even in the brightest moments the skies seem dark, everything about this salad feels like a welcome breath of fresh air: the riotous clashing colors of the sunshine orange and deep pink beets, as well as the lightness and sharp freshness of the flavors. There is no reason, of course, why you should confine yourself to eating this salad only in the winter months, rather what I mean to say is that winter tends to be when I appreciate it most, at that point of the year when fresh fruit and vegetables are so much harder to come by and so very limited by way of choice. For ease and simplicity I use cooked beets, the kind you buy vacuum-packed from the supermarket, but if instead you prefer to cook them yourself, roast them whole in an oven heated to 400°F with just a drizzle of olive oil and salt for 45 minutes, until firm but tender. Once cool, rub the skins off with paper towels and slice into rounds.

HANDS ON TIME:
10 minutes
SERVES 2

2 cooked beets (total
   weight about 6oz)
2 small oranges, pith and
   peel removed
1 tbsp olive oil
½ tbsp apple cider vinegar
½ cup crumbled feta cheese
flaky sea salt and freshly
   ground black pepper

Slice the beets and the oranges into rounds, each ¼ inch thick. Arrange them on a serving dish: I like to do this in concentric circles with the slices overlapping, but feel free to arrange it on the plate as you think it looks prettiest.

In a small bowl, lightly whisk the olive oil and vinegar together and drizzle over the salad.

Scatter the feta over the orange and beets and season to taste with salt and pepper.

Fregola Sarda with Seafood

Fregola is a Sardinian pasta that comes in the shape of little pea-sized balls; you'll sometimes see it in shops labeled as Italian or Sardinian couscous. If you can't find it, then giant couscous will do very well (though follow the cooking instructions on the package). Typically you serve it with seafood, which is how I've prepared it here, in a light, colorful dish dressed with cherry tomatoes and a generous dash of white wine. I've used frozen seafood in this recipe, rather than fresh from the seafood market, simply for ease; I keep bags of it in the freezer and take disproportionate delight in the fact that doing so means I can improvise this sort of sumptuous supper effortlessly and at the last minute.

HANDS ON TIME:
15 minutes
SERVES 2

2 vegetable bouillon cubes
heaping 1 cup fregola sarda
3 tbsp olive oil
1⅓ cups cherry or grape
   tomatoes, halved
10oz frozen mixed seafood
3 tbsp white wine
leaves from a small bunch
   of parsley, chopped
flaky sea salt and freshly
   ground black pepper

Bring a large saucepan of generously salted water to a boil. When the water begins to gallop, crumble in the bouillon cubes and give it a good stir to dissolve them. Now add the fregola and cook for 6–8 minutes. Drain the grains in a colander and set to one side.

Meanwhile, heat 2 tbsp olive oil in a large frying pan, then toss in half the tomatoes and cook over a high heat for 2–3 minutes, until they begin to cook down. Now add the frozen seafood and cook for 6–8 minutes to thaw it fully.

Pour in the wine, add the last of the tomatoes and the parsley and cook for 1–2 minutes, just long enough for the new batch of tomatoes to tenderize slightly and for some of the juices to cook off. Add the cooked fregola to the pan and give everything a good stir to combine.

Keep the pan over a high heat until warmed through, then take off the heat, drizzle over the last 1 tbsp olive oil, then season to taste with a little salt and a good grinding of pepper before serving.

Black Truffle and Cheese Omelet

Omelet is something I often cook for myself, as it's quick, easy and perfectly portioned for a single person. Cheese omelet decorated and infused with slivers of black truffle, on the other hand, is for date nights, for pretty much all the same reasons but with the added specialness of the truffle. And truffles are indeed special: I buy them in small jars online and save them for occasions such as this. Each omelet is perfect for one person: you can either cook them in quick succession using a single pan, or have two burners going simultaneously. As to how much truffle to adorn the omelet with, that's really up to you... This recipe contains lightly cooked eggs, so take all the usual precautions, if you need to do so (see page 70).

HANDS ON TIME:
15 minutes
SERVES 2

4 eggs
2 tsp olive oil
⅔ cup grated Cheddar
  cheese
10–20 slices of black
  truffle, depending on
  taste and budget
flaky sea salt and freshly
  ground black pepper

Crack the eggs into a mixing bowl and season with a pinch of salt and some pepper. Beat well with a fork.

Heat 1 tsp olive oil in a medium-small frying pan (I use an 8-inch pan) over a medium heat, then pour in half the eggs. Tilt the pan to spread them out evenly, using a fork to spread the eggs around the pan a little if you need to. After 1–2 minutes, when the omelet begins to cook and firm up but still has a little raw egg on top, sprinkle over half the cheese and dot 5–10 truffle slices over it.

Use a spatula to ease the edges of the omelet away from the pan, then fold it over in half, as if closing a book.

Cook for another minute or so, and when it starts to turn golden brown underneath, remove the pan from the heat and slide the omelet on to a plate. Make a second omelet with the remaining ingredients.

Anthony's Special Crêpes

🎁 *You can store the crêpe batter in the fridge in a jar sealed with its lid (or in an empty glass bottle) for up to two days. Then just fry them up when you want to eat them; make sure to include cooking instructions.*

This is Anthony's recipe for crêpes, relayed here quasi verbatim. And so I must also include his insistence that the art of the perfect crêpe lies in getting the right heat on the pan: too cold and you won't get a nice color; too hot and they'll blister. He firmly advocates patience before adding that first splash of batter: breathe and wait to make sure that the pan is hot enough. And then, as you keep frying them, if at any point it feels like they're burning, take the pan off the heat to cool for a few moments between crêpes, to regulate the temperature; wipe any burning butter off the pan with paper towels and start again. Anthony also likes to have two pans on the go at the same time, so he can make them faster and so that the crêpes are still warm by the time he sits down to eat them.

As to how to eat them, that really is my field of expertise: I like mine with lemon juice and sugar, as recommended here, but you could of course try anything from preserves to chocolate-hazelnut spread to honey and a few sliced almonds. I like them for breakfast, just as I like them for dessert after a special meal.

You will find the quantities here are more than generous for two people, but with crêpes you want the luxury of being able to always help yourself to more, so I prefer to err on the side of excess. Either keep any leftover batter in the fridge and make more crêpes fresh the next day, or, if you have any leftover crêpes, you can spread a generous dollop of chocolate-hazelnut spread all over one side (and add a few slices of banana too, if you like), then fold the rounds into fat triangles. Arrange the chocolate-laden crêpes overlapping in a baking dish and drizzle over a little melted butter, a smattering of sliced almonds and/or a sprinkle of granulated sugar, then bake in an oven heated to 400°F for 10 minutes or so, just long enough to warm them. It makes for the most indulgently good dessert. Surely that's a reason alone for leftovers?

HANDS ON TIME:
30 minutes
HANDS OFF TIME:
overnight resting (if you
can), or 10 minutes (if
pressed for time)
SERVES 2, with some
leftovers

scant 1¼ cups all-purpose
  flour
2 eggs
1 cup plus 2 tbsp whole
  milk
1 heaping tsp salted butter,
  softened, plus more for
  the pan
flaky sea salt
lemon juice, to serve
granulated sugar, to serve

Combine the flour, eggs, milk, softened butter and a pinch
of salt in a blender and blitz until just mixed (take care not
to over-blitz or it will stretch the gluten and make the
crêpes overly chewy), then chill the batter in the fridge
overnight, or at least for a few hours. Alternatively, if
you're pressed for time, you can just leave the batter to sit
at room temperature for 10 minutes or so, just long
enough to allow any remaining clumps of flour to dissolve.

If you let the batter rest overnight you will need
to mix it up again a little before cooking. Melt a little
butter in a non-stick frying pan (an 8-inch pan will give
you 9–10 crêpes) over a medium heat.

When the pan is hot but not burning, add a ladleful
of crêpe batter and jiggle the pan a little so it spreads out
over the whole base. When little bubbles begin to appear
on the surface, give the pan a little shake and flip the
crêpe. Fry for 30–60 seconds on the second side, until
lightly golden.

Repeat the same process with the remaining crêpe
batter. Serve with lemon juice and granulated sugar.

Nutella Tiramisù

Pile high in old-fashioned glasses or glass jars and cover with parchment paper tied with twine (or seal with the jar's lid). It will keep in the fridge for two or three days.

Tiramisù was the first thing I ever cooked – aged nineteen – for my husband, not long after we first met. And still, twenty years on, I cling to the romantic notion that my tiramisù is how and why he first fell in love with me. The recipe I use today is that same, untouched and unchanged in all these years because I genuinely don't think it can be improved upon; but this version is slightly tweaked to include lashings of Nutella between each layer of coffee-soaked savoiardi and whipped mascarpone cream. The chocolate-hazelnut spread, infused with coffee, turns almost fudgy once chilled in the fridge and is outrageously good. By the same principle, you could make the tiramisù with a dollop of Pistachio Butter (see page 215) in place of the chocolate or – for true, over-the-top indulgence – as well as. This recipe contains raw eggs, so take all the usual precautions, if you need to do so (see page 70).

HANDS ON TIME:
20 minutes
HANDS OFF TIME:
30 minutes in the fridge
(if you can)
SERVES 2

1 egg
2 tbsp superfine sugar
½ cup mascarpone, at room
    temperature
6–8 savoiardi (ladyfinger)
    cookies
¼ cup strong coffee, cooled
¼ cup chocolate-hazelnut
    spread, such as Nutella
unsweetened cocoa
    powder, to dust

Start by separating the egg. In a spotlessly clean mixing bowl, whisk the white with a hand-held electric mixer. As it begins to froth, add half the sugar, a spoon at a time, until it forms glossy white peaks, then set to one side.

In a second mixing bowl, whisk the yolk with the rest of the sugar until it doubles in volume and become a light, soft lemony color. Now spoon the mascarpone into the yolk and beat until smooth and creamy. Gently fold in the egg white, trying to keep as much of the air as possible in the cream.

Arrange half the savoiardi in a single layer in each glass or small serving bowl, breaking them into smaller pieces if you need to. Drizzle a little coffee over them, enough to soak them generously, then spoon a dollop of chocolate-hazelnut spread on top and use the back of the spoon to spread it out as evenly as you can. If it is tricky to spread, you can try warming it in a microwave for 20 seconds beforehand, to just soften it; otherwise, spoon it in clumps, it matters little if it isn't evenly distributed and will taste glorious either way. Top with a good dollop of mascarpone cream and spread out until the chocolate is completely hidden under a blanket of cream. Repeat with a second layer of savoiardi, coffee, chocolate-hazelnut spread and mascarpone cream, then dust lightly with cocoa powder.

Chill in the fridge for at least 30 minutes (if you can) before serving.

Chocolate and Rosemary Tart

🎁 *These will keep happily in the fridge for two or three days, stored in a cake box or airtight container, or quite simply on a plate covered with reusable food wrap.*

One of my greatest pleasures in life is cookbooks: I devour them with possibly even greater greed than I do the food that graces their pages. I love the stories; I love planning one day what I'll cook the next, and for whom; I love reading the books in bed like storybooks, filled with pictures that transport me to another world. One of my most loved and worn cookbooks is Nikki Segnit's *The Flavor Thesaurus*, which sits on my bedside table, its rainbow-striped cover now faded and decorated with rings where mugs of tea have rested lazily upon it. Within that cover lies a culinary treasure trove of tales and inspiration, including the recipe for David Wilson's little chocolate and rosemary pots, which was the starting point for this tart: buttery, fine shortcrust pastry (I use good store-bought for ease and simplicity) brimming with velvety-rich chocolate cream laced with white wine and just a whisper of rosemary. The result is positively ambrosial: silky-smooth, almost like caramel on your tongue and so divinely scented it transports you to a happy, magical land you never want to leave. The recipe below caters for two, and I tend for ease to make it as two individual tarts, partly because they look so very pretty on the plate, but do feel free to increase the quantities and bake as a single large tart for occasions when you're catering to a crowd.

HANDS ON TIME:
30 minutes
HANDS OFF TIME:
25–35 minutes in the oven;
1 hour in the fridge
SERVES 2

1 x 8-inch store-bought
   refrigerated pie crust
   (from a 14.1-oz package)
¼ cup superfine sugar
3 tbsp white wine
½ cup heavy cream
1 rosemary sprig
1½oz bittersweet chocolate,
   very finely chopped
rosemary flowers,
   to decorate, if you
   grow the herb
   (obviously optional!)

Heat the oven to 350°F. Line two 4-inch tart pans with pastry. Prick the bottom of the tart crusts all over with a fork, then cover with parchment paper, fill with baking beans and blind-bake for 20–25 minutes until lightly colored at the edges. Remove the parchment and the beans, then set the pans back in the oven and bake for a further 5–10 minutes, until lightly golden all over.

Meanwhile, combine the sugar and wine in a small, heavy-based saucepan. Heat gently until the sugar has dissolved, stirring occasionally. Stir in the cream, add the rosemary sprig and cook gently until warmed. Add the chocolate and bring to a boil, stirring until the chocolate has melted.

Now reduce the heat and simmer for 20 minutes, until the mixture becomes very dark. At this point, remove and discard the rosemary sprig and pour the sweet-scented chocolate cream into the tart crusts.

Chill in the fridge for 1 hour or so before serving, with rosemary flowers scattered on top, if you like.

Rhubarb Syllabub

This is a sherbet-y, light creamy confection, neither too sweet nor too rich, more tangy than anything else, almost like really good Greek yogurt. For me, it's all about the fuchsia-pink swirls, which, set against the quasi-virginal purity of the thick white cream, remind me in some way of the hand-marbled papers they sell in old stationery shops in Venice. I like to serve this in a glass, or a glass bowl, so that you can see the sunset of pinks clearly: you can either pile the syllabub high and serve in a single glass to share, or, if you prefer, divide it into two smaller, individual portions. I tend to serve this as is, but if you feel it needs a little something extra, perhaps offer a few shortbread cookies on the side: good, store-bought shortbread, or my Rose and Cinnamon Shortbread (see page 235) would work a treat with the rhubarb and is both simple and quick to make. Both syllabub and shortbread can be prepared well in advance.

HANDS ON TIME:
20 minutes
HANDS OFF TIME:
20 minutes in the fridge
SERVES 2 very generously

4 thin stalks rhubarb, cut
    into small chunks (about
    1¾ cups)
2 tbsp granulated sugar
scant 1 cup heavy cream
2 tbsp brandy

Put the rhubarb in a small saucepan with the sugar. Set over a gentle heat and cook slowly for 15 minutes, stirring every so often, until soft. Take off the heat and mash the fruit a little with a wooden spoon, to break it up. Leave to cool.

In a clean mixing bowl, whip the cream until stiff, taking care not to over-whip it. Add the brandy and whip once more to combine.

Gently fold the poached rhubarb through the cream and spoon the candy-floss pink concoction into 1 or 2 glasses, depending on how you want to serve it.

Chill in the fridge for at least 20 minutes, then serve the syllabub as is, or with a couple of pieces of Rose and Cinnamon Shortbread.

Baileys Pannacotta

Set in old-fashioned glasses or glass jars and cover with parchment paper tied with twine (or seal with the jar's lid). It keeps in the fridge for two or three days.

Part of the charm of pannacotta is that you can make it well in advance and just have it sitting. quivering. in the fridge until you are ready to serve it. All of which makes it a very practical dessert for a first date, or indeed for any date. There is something innately seductive about the silky texture of the sweetened chilled cream. its honeyed caramel color and the generous splash of fiery Baileys that goes into it: this is undoubtedly a grown-up dessert.

HANDS ON TIME:
10 minutes
HANDS OFF TIME:
4+ hours in the fridge
SERVES 2

1¼ tsp unflavored gelatin
    powder
1¼ cups heavy cream
heaping ¼ cup superfine
    sugar
5 tbsp Baileys Original
    Irish Cream liqueur
unsweetened cocoa
    powder. to dust
    (optional)

Put 1 tbsp water in a small heatproof bowl, sprinkle over the powdered gelatin and set aside to hydrate.

Combine the cream and sugar together in a small, heavy-based saucepan and set over a medium-low heat. Just before the cream comes to a boil (you will see the tiniest bubbles begin to form at the edge of the pan), take the pan off the heat.

Add ¼ cup of the warmed cream to the gelatin and stir until the gelatin has completely dissolved, then add this mixture to the saucepan of warm cream and stir until combined. Now pour in the Baileys and stir until smooth.

Pour the liquid into 2 glasses or molds and set in the fridge for at least 4 hours, until completely set. Dust with a little cocoa powder before serving. if you like.

Toblerone Fondue

I can't tell you how much I love this recipe: it's simple really, a pool of melted chocolate mixed with just a dash of cream, with fresh fruit for dipping. You could of course adopt the same principle and make this with plain bittersweet – or indeed even milk – chocolate, and that would be very fine thing indeed; but melting Toblerone instead gives the fondue an especially velvety texture, with shards of chewy, toffee-like nougat, honeyed and sweet, in the dipping sauce. The sauce is perfectly fine at room temperature, but especially nice warm, so if you want to make it in advance (and I probably would) you can leave it resting in its pan on the stove, then just before serving set it over a low heat for a few minutes, just long enough to warm it through like hot chocolate, then pour into a bowl. Serve with fruit for dipping: strawberries and other berries, of course, but also physalis and even sliced, peeled citrus, chunks of white peach in summer, and – my particular favorite – sweet chips of dried apple, mango or fig.

HANDS ON TIME:
10 minutes
SERVES 2

⅓ cup heavy cream
2 x 3.5-oz milk chocolate
    Toblerone bars, or 7oz of
    your favorite chocolate,
    finely chopped
flaky sea salt
fresh or dried fruits,
    to serve

Warm the cream in a small saucepan over a medium-low heat. Just before it begins to boil, when you see the tiniest bubbles rising up at the edge of the pan, take the pan off the heat and add the chocolate. Stir until the chocolate is melted and you have a velvety smooth sauce with shards of nougat. Add a generous pinch of salt and stir it in.

Pour the warm sauce into a small bowl and serve with fresh and/or dried fruits.

Spiced Oranges with Brandy and Sugar

🎁 *These will keep happily in an airtight container in the fridge for two or three days.*

How utterly and almost ridiculously simple this dish is to prepare shouldn't take away from what a pleasure it is to eat: sweet, juicy slices of orange swimming in a syrup of brandy, intermingled with a little fresh juice from the fruit, warming cinnamon and just a dash of caramel-like sugar. It's simple, but sophisticated, which is exactly what I long for in date-night food. You could of course serve it with some lightly whipped cream on the side, if you like, and spoon that over the oranges before eating... but honestly, it's hardly needed: the ambrosial flavor of the fruit with that hint of booziness is more than enough.

HANDS ON TIME:
5 minutes
HANDS OFF TIME:
1 hour, or up to overnight, to macerate
SERVES 2

2 oranges, preferably
   navel variety
2 heaping tbsp granulated
   sugar
2 tbsp brandy
¼ tsp ground cinnamon,
   plus a little more
   to serve

Peel the oranges and remove their pith, then slice into ½-inch thick rounds. Toss the orange slices in a dish along with all the other ingredients.

Cover and let macerate in the fridge for at least 1 hour, or overnight if you prefer.

Dust with a little more cinnamon before serving chilled from the fridge.

Flourless Chocolate and Espresso Cakes

❦ I like to bake these as individual cakes in small heart-shaped pans, if for no other reason than I'm a hopeless romantic and have a soft spot for the happy cheesiness of heart-shaped baked goods. But don't feel that you have to do the same: you could of course bake two individual chocolate cakes in little round pans, or you could double the quantities and bake a large cake in a standard 9-inch pan, then serve a generous slice, plated, dusted lightly in confectioners' sugar and with a dollop of sour cream on the side; keep the rest to enjoy as leftovers over the coming days, as it's one of those cakes that will happily store in an airtight container for three or four days.

The recipe here is an adaptation of Emiko Davies's recipe for *torta caprese*, a kind of flourless chocolate cake – indulgently gooey in the middle and crisp on top – that hails from the sunshine-drenched Amalfi coast. To Emiko's recipe, here barely adapted, I've added a healthy dose of ground coffee powder: the coffee intensifies the richness and darkness of the chocolate, resulting in a wonderfully grown-up cake.

HANDS ON TIME:
15 minutes
HANDS OFF TIME:
20–25 minutes in the oven
SERVES 2

3 tbsp (45g) salted butter, chopped, plus more for the tins
2oz (50g) bittersweet chocolate, finely chopped
1 heaping tbsp instant espresso powder
½ cup (50g) almond meal
1 egg
¼ cup (50g) superfine sugar
confectioners' sugar, to dust (optional)
sour cream and raspberries, to serve (optional)

Heat the oven to 325°F. Butter two 4-inch heart-shaped or round springform pans and line them both with parchment paper.

In a small saucepan, melt the butter and chocolate together over a very low heat. Once the chocolate is completely melted, stir in the espresso powder, take the pan off the heat and add the almond meal.

Separate the egg. In a spotlessly clean bowl, whisk the white and, as it begins to froth, add half the superfine sugar a spoonful at a time, whisking all the while, until you have a glossy and stiff white mass, like meringue. In a second bowl, whisk the yolk together with the remaining superfine sugar until it has doubled in volume and turned a pale, creamy shade of yellow. Gently fold the white into the yolk, then fold in the melted chocolate mixture.

Divide the cake batter equally between the prepared pans and bake for 20–25 minutes. The cakes should be dry on top and feel firm to the touch. To test if they're done, insert a toothpick or knife to the middle: it won't come out completely clean, but the cake should be crumby rather than liquid.

Leave to cool for at least 10 minutes in the pans and serve either warm or at room temperature, dusted with confectioners' sugar and/or with sour cream or raspberries, as you like.

White Chocolate and Pistachio Tortini

🎁 *These will keep in the freezer in their little ramekins for three months. Make sure to include a note with baking instructions, if you're dropping them off as a gift.*

A wonderfully fudgy dessert somehow in the same family as sticky toffee pudding. The *tortino* or 'little cake' is made from white chocolate, which gives it that intensely dense texture, then baked at its center is a dollop of melting sweet pistachio cream. This you can buy in jars – most Italian delicatessens or specialist online suppliers stock it – or make for yourself following my recipe (see page 215). I love white chocolate and pistachio together, but you could equally substitute a dollop of chocolate-hazelnut spread for the pistachio cream. Once prepared, these need to rest in the freezer for a few hours, so you do need to think ahead; but on the flip side you can make them in advance and have them ready to put in the oven when needed.

HANDS ON TIME:
20 minutes

HANDS OFF TIME:
3 hours in the freezer;
25 minutes in the oven

SERVES 2

7 tbsp salted butter, plus more for the ramekins

4oz white chocolate, finely chopped

heaping ¼ cup superfine sugar

2 eggs

2 level tbsp all-purpose flour

2 heaping tsp Pistachio Butter (see page 215), store-bought pistachio cream, or chocolate-hazelnut spread

confectioners' sugar, to dust (optional)

finely chopped pistachios, to serve (optional)

Butter two 4-inch ramekins, making sure to liberally coat the bases.

Combine the white chocolate, butter and sugar in a small saucepan and set over a low heat to melt. Stir regularly to stop the chocolate from catching and take the pan off the heat as soon as it is melted.

In a small bowl, lightly beat the eggs with a fork. Add the eggs to the melted chocolate and stir vigorously until well combined. Now add the flour to the chocolate and stir vigorously until you have a smooth, chocolatey cream.

Pour one-quarter of the mixture into each of the prepared ramekins. Spoon a dollop of Pistachio Butter, pistachio cream or chocolate-hazelnut spread into the middle of each, then pour over the remaining chocolate mix, dividing it equally between each ramekin so the pistachio or chocolate is completely covered.

Cover and set in the freezer for a couple of hours (longer if you like).

When you are ready to serve, heat the oven to 400°F.

Bake the *tortini* straight from the freezer, in the middle of the oven, for 25 minutes, until lightly golden on top and slightly risen in the middle. They should feel firm to the touch. Dust with confectioners' sugar and/or a scattering of pistachios, if you like, before serving while still warm.

NOURISH

Some thoughts on unconditional love, and recipes for all the family

Before I had children, I thought I'd enjoy nothing more than to cook for them. In my mind's eye we would live out a sequence of halcyon meals, these imaginary children and I; life was going to be filled with cookies, milk and chat, general jolliness and 'gee whizz this is good'. But, as with so much of parenting, the reality has proved different. Not better, not worse, just different.

One thing I'd failed to consider is that, once you have children, you're blessed with less time for cooking, not more. The other – and this really did come as a surprise to me – is that parenting can be lonely, even when you have a partner to share the load with, and even though, counterintuitive as it might seem, once you have children there are more of you to the family, not fewer. The early years can be most especially lonely, before your children grow into the people you love so much because of who they are rather than solely because they're your children, and before you share so much – interest, life and history – in common.

The cooking can also be lonely. So much of what I love about cooking is to feel as though I am bringing joy to the people I cook for... and yet what I soon discovered, when I became a mother, is that your efforts in the kitchen are rarely received with much by way of fanfare. I've since realized that cooking for your family is about knowing that you're doing something good rather than being told you're doing something good. Again, there's nothing better or worse about this, it's just different from what I imagined.

This chapter, in contrast with the previous one, is about cooking for those people you know really well, possibly even too well. It's about a more mature kind of love, a love the Greeks called *Storge*: that's unconditional, stoic, familiar, deep and – above all – everlasting.

It ought to be the easiest chapter for me to write because, as the mother of two boys, Aeneas and Achille, this kind of catering is the metaphorical bread and butter of my culinary life. And yet, this is also the kind of cooking that most often feels like a chore. I find it easy to enjoy the rigmarole of Christmas lunch, because it only comes about once a year, and its celebratory novelty value makes it wonderfully fun; but cooking every day for an audience that often feels unappreciative can prove more of a challenge, not just logistically (how will I find the time?) but also emotionally (how will I find the strength?).

I was lucky enough to grow up in a home where food was equated with love; that opened up for me a world of pleasure which has enriched my life profoundly, and for which I will forever be grateful. The dining table was not just where we ate, but where we as a family learned, shared and grew; I, as the youngest, perhaps most especially so.

Nowadays I look back nostalgically on the breakfasts, lunches and dinners which were the happy chorus of my childhood, but at the time I didn't give it much thought. Children who don't know any different take things for granted, and I try to remember this now that I am a mother myself: both how much pleasure the food that colored my childhood (and the rituals that surround it) has brought me, but also how long I took to recognize that.

I try to think of the bigger picture, most especially in those moments of despondence, frustration or exhaustion (and there are enough of those). How and what we eat when we are little, in some way or another, stays with us for the rest of our lives, so to be the initial architect of a person's attitude to food is the very greatest privilege.

I insist upon this point, because it is possible that no one else is going to remind you that, when you make a pasta for lunch or some kind of sheet pan dinner, you are doing an important job. In fact, a very important job. Remembering this keeps me going when no one likes what I've cooked, and I'm rushed and tired, and it all just feels a bit hopeless (which it often does). And I hope that you will remember it too, on the tougher days as well as the good days, because there are lots of good days.

As parents, because we want the very best for our children, we set expectations sky-high, which is why so often, too often, we feel as though we have failed. So I want here to place an emphasis on the 'simple': yes, I believe cooking for your family is a hugely worthwhile investment of precious resources, but I also believe you don't need to be a skilled cook to cook well. Fresh ingredients – seasonal if you can – simply, very simply prepared, is the best way

(I have found, at least) of getting food on the table that you and your family are excited to eat, while juggling the impossibly busy business of the rest of your life.

Simple things, small tricks that make all the difference: tossing some green beans or a few florets of broccoli into the cooking water with your pasta when you're making pesto (this adds flavor and texture, but also makes more of a proper – not to mention nutritious – meal of it); or using store-bought pie crust for a tart, so all you need to do is top it with whatever you have kicking around (tomatoes, black olives and cheese are my go-to) and put in the oven to bake; and so on... These are small, quick, easy solutions to dinner that, once you get into the habit of them, become intuitive and I find really help.

And then for those days when even that feels too herculean an effort, there are always fish sticks. My own childhood was happily awash with fish sticks and I can see my sons' going that way too.

In these pages, you'll find the kind of simple recipes I like to think of as 'everyday jeans' cooking: as much as I might splash out occasionally on a party dress, to find a pair of perfect jeans – hardwearing, flattering, with pockets in just the right places – is the real sartorial holy grail, it makes a tangible difference to your daily life.

Just as everyday clothes must be comfortable, these recipes are too; the benchmark being what can I get on the table quickly, with a toddler howling at me. Not the most elegant criterion, perhaps, but very true to life. Some recipes here are quicker and easier to make than others (though the tomato pasta, especially, is a godsend when speed is of the essence), but all the recipes here fall loosely under this umbrella.

These dishes are all firm favorites in our household. I know everyone's tastes are different; just because Aeneas's favorite thing in the world is pasta al pesto, it doesn't mean it need be either yours or your family's, or indeed that it will still be his in two months' time (he can be fickle). But I can't really think of a better reason to pass on a recipe than because you truly love it, so, if the recipe is in here, that is why: because we all love it and we cook it often.

What I haven't attempted is to cater for fussy eaters;
I offer no strategies for hiding vegetables in cake or for
making dinner into something that resembles a smiley face
(though I have heard both these tricks work well). I believe
that if you feed children lots of flavors at a young age, if
you enjoy your food and can transmit that enthusiasm to
those around you, then your children will enjoy eating just
as you do.

This might take time, but it will happen. Aeneas and
Achille week on week develop new culinary whims, likes
and dislikes (currently: onions and lemon for Aeneas and
basil for Achille, all of which will have changed by the time
you read this). I try to relax into it: I neither pander to their
tastes nor force them to agree with mine; I hold tight to
those precious moments when Aeneas rates my risotto a
9/10 (high praise indeed) or Achille polishes his plate.
I also discourage both boys from snacking, so they are
hungry when we sit down (this really helps). Dinner is what
it is, and no one is offered alternatives. I make a point of *not*
saying 'eat this because it's good for you', because I have
never suddenly wanted to eat something purely because I'm
told it's good for me. But I do often say, 'try this, I think
you'll like it', because while I didn't perhaps enjoy broccoli,
avocado or salad so much as a child (in fact, I remember
loathing them), I delight in them now. I don't insist the boys
eat everything on their plate, but I do encourage them to try
at least one bite of everything. If food is an expression of
love, it seems only fair to ask that the gesture be
acknowledged. And credit to the boys, they mostly
understand this, and they do their best. As do I.

I love to cook with my two boys, who are now ten and
three years old. Largely we do this because it is fun, and
many of the recipes in this chapter are those we cook
together. The desserts, for example, in the pages that follow
are all simple enough that you can bake them with your own
children and my hope is that you will find it very rewarding
to do so; the same goes for many of the savory dishes, such
as polpette, bread pizza or tomato and cheese tart.

Cooking with small children is perhaps not for every day,
when there's homework to wrangle with and bath time to

negotiate, but for rainy Saturdays or Sundays, when wholesome activities need to be dreamed up to keep everyone entertained. Not only is it a genuinely pleasurable way to spend time together, but it comes with the bonus that, at the end of it all, you'll have dinner made. (Though I'll admit that it can take a while to restore order to the kitchen in the aftermath.) The pride on the boys' faces when we all sit down to eat something they have made encapsulates in miniature everything this book is about.

I've found that involving my children in cooking has helped them learn how to enjoy eating: they are always curious about what we've made, and proud to share it. Beyond that, taking part in the process helps them grow an understanding of where food comes from, and the effort implicit in preparing it. I don't want to paint too chocolate-box a picture of all this, mind you, because while cooking with my boys has been one of the great joys of watching them grow up, it does come with the caveat that things never pan out quite as you planned. Sometimes (often) they'll lose interest halfway through, and they always make a mess. It's chaotic, and by no means the most efficient way of getting a meal on the table, but it creates little moments of joy and, like anything in life, the more often we do it together, the better we are at it.

Most importantly, I want to emphasize that while this is a chapter largely about cooking for children, these recipes are intended for everyone, of all ages. I never like to draw a distinction between children's food and grown-up food: at home, we all enjoy the same menu, and experience the same flavors. I'm not going to pretend that our family meals are perfect, that there are never tears or sullen conversation, but we do eat together, just as we live together and grow together, and, on balance, somehow it all works out that the good moments far and beyond outweigh any sticky ones. It's certainly not a perfect recipe for anything, but it's as close as I've got.

Pasta with Pesto and Extra Greens

This tastes just as good at room temperature as it does warm, so it's ideal for picnics and doorstep drop-offs. Store in an airtight container in the fridge for up to two days.

I rarely bother making pesto, unless it's Pistachio Pesto (see page 220); I tend to buy a good, oily version from my local grocer. Still, I've included a recipe for pesto below, in case you feel like making it – it's not tricky – or have lots of basil in your garden that you want to use up (it freezes nicely, if needed).

The classic recipe, made with basil, pine nuts and lots of Parmesan, is Ligurian pesto (as opposed to the aforementioned pistachio variety, which hails from Sicily), and in Liguria they cook pasta with green beans and baby potatoes, then toss the lot in creamy, sweet-scented pesto. My version has no potatoes, but a mix of broccoli, green beans and sweet fennel (sometimes zucchini, fava beans or romanesco broccoli). It truly is a one-pot dish, and a guaranteed way of persuading my boys to enjoy a meal brimming with bright greens. Cooking times vary depending on the kind of pasta and greens you go for: short pasta works best, and chop the veggies into pieces roughly the same size as the pasta so the two cook evenly. You will need a surprisingly big pot, so use the largest you have.

HANDS ON TIME:
20 minutes
SERVES 4

FOR THE PESTO
5 cups basil leaves
⅔ cup olive oil, plus more
   to serve
¼ cup pine nuts
scant 1 cup grated
   Parmesan cheese, or
   pecorino, plus more
   to serve
flaky sea salt

FOR THE PASTA
14oz fusilli
¼ head broccoli, handful
   of green beans and ½
   fennel bulb, all chopped
   into pasta-sized pieces

To make the pesto, combine the basil, olive oil and pine nuts in a food processor and blitz until you have a grassy mixture, then add the cheese and blitz again to combine into a creamy, verdant green sauce. You want to blitz everything for as short a time as possible so as to keep the bright color of the sauce. Season to taste with salt.

Fill the largest saucepan you have with cold water, salt very generously and bring to a boil. When the water begins to gallop, add the pasta and cook *al dente*, following the package instructions. For fusilli, this should take roughly 10 minutes. After 5 minutes, add the vegetables to the pan too, and cook everything together. When the pasta is cooked, scoop a cup of the cooking water out and set to one side.

Drain the pasta and the veggies together in a colander, then toss back into their pan. Add the pesto sauce along with a splash of the reserved cooking water and give everything a good stir, so all the greens and the pasta are coated in a creamy gloss of pesto.

Serve immediately, with more Parmesan or pecorino and a drizzle of olive oil.

Pasta alla Bibi

⊞ *Spoon the sauce into a glass jar and store in the fridge for up to one week. Drop off with a bag of good pasta and cooking instructions.*

When I was pregnant with our second son, Achille, our eldest reverentially named my bump 'Baby Brother'; no 'my' before it, just 'Baby Brother'. 'Baby Brother is getting big,' he would say. 'How many weeks until Baby Brother will be here?' Round about month five, it was shortened to 'BB', which in turn became 'Bibi'. By the time Achille was born, he was – and forever will be – Bibi.

We call this recipe 'pasta alla Bibi' because it's Achille's favorite, and because my husband came up with the recipe on one particularly challenging afternoon while minding both boys. Its genius lies in the fact that you can make a fresh tomato sauce in the time it takes water to come to a boil and pasta to cook, without needing everything to simmer for-seeming-ever, or to stir and hover over the pan obsessively. You just throw everything in, add a splash of water to stop the tomatoes from burning, then let the ingredients fend for themselves, freeing you up to tend to a toddler's every whim and demand. Or indeed to do whatever else it is you might want to do.

Essentially, it's a super-simple tomato sauce, but a very good one and magically quick to make. My only insistence is that you include the butter at the end: it somehow mellows the acidity of the tomatoes and is what gives the sauce an almost creamy flavor.

HANDS ON TIME:

15 minutes

SERVES 4

14oz pasta; any kind
will do, but spaghetti is
my favorite

6 cups cherry or grape
tomatoes

3 tbsp salted butter

½ cup grated Parmesan
cheese, plus more
to serve

flaky sea salt and freshly
ground black pepper

olive oil, to serve

Put a large saucepan of generously salted water on to boil.
When the water begins to gallop, add the pasta and cook
al dente, following the package instructions.

When you put the water on to boil, take a medium-
sized saucepan and pour in ½ inch (roughly) of cold water;
add the tomatoes whole and as is. Set over a high heat
and bring to a boil. Leave to bubble away. Check on the
tomatoes every now and then and give them a stir: if the
pan is looking dry, then take a ladleful of water from the
pasta pan and add to the tomatoes to stop them sticking
on the bottom. By the time the pasta is cooked, you should
have a chunky tomato sauce. If the tomatoes haven't all
burst, you can squash them a little with the back of your
wooden spoon.

Take the tomatoes off the heat, add the butter and
Parmesan and stir in until melted. Season to taste with
a little salt and a few good grindings of pepper.

Scoop a cup of the pasta water out of the saucepan
and set to one side. When the pasta is cooked, drain in a
colander and toss back in the pan. Add the tomato sauce
and a splash of the reserved cooking water and stir
together so all the pasta is coated in sauce.

Serve immediately with more Parmesan, olive oil and
salt, to taste.

Pasta con Panna e Piselli

Pasta cooked this way, swimming in a sauce of cream, juicy almost-sugar-sweet peas and freshly ground black pepper, is one of my strongest happy memories from childhood. And I still love to eat it now. It's one of those effortless dishes that everyone loves: effortless in the sense that it's quick and easy to make of course, but effortless also in the sense that the flavors are innately comforting, intuitive to enjoy at all stages of life. If you wanted, you could fry some cubed pancetta with the onion and add it, salty and dripping with fat, to the white creamy sauce. Or you might want to add a dash of ground saffron to the cream to give it extra warmth, color and a punch of flavor, so evocative of dreamy holidays in a far exotic land as much as of familiar nursery food.

One word on pasta shapes: this is one of those sauces that works well with all shapes, though convention would stipulate a short pasta of some kind, be it penne or fusilli or rigatoni or what have you, rather than spaghetti or linguine (though if that's what you have to hand, use it). I have a soft spot for farfalle, the little butterflies, if only because it's such a joyful, playful shape.

HANDS ON TIME:
25 minutes
SERVES 4

2 tbsp olive oil
1 onion, finely chopped
2 heaping cups frozen peas
½ vegetable bouillon cube
10oz farfalle, or another
    (ideally short) pasta
1 cup heavy cream
flaky sea salt and freshly
    ground black pepper
Parmesan cheese, grated,
    to serve

Bring a large saucepan of generously salted water to a boil.

Heat the oil in a large frying pan – large enough to hold the cooked pasta – over a medium-low heat. Add the onion with a pinch of salt and cook for 3–5 minutes, until soft and translucent. Tip the peas into the pan with the onion, giving everything a good stir. Add a ladleful of the salted water from the pasta saucepan, crumble in the half bouillon cube, increase the heat and cook for 10–15 minutes, until the liquid has cooked right down and the peas taste sweet and are almost mushy in texture.

Meanwhile add the pasta to the pan of boiling water, which should by now be at a galloping boil, and cook *al dente*, following the package instructions.

Pour the cream into the pan with the peas, give everything a good stir and reduce the heat. Cook gently for a few minutes to warm the cream all the way through.

Drain the pasta, reserving a cup of the cooking water. Toss the pasta into the pan with the peas and a splash of the reserved cooking water. Mix everything together so all the pasta is coated in the creamy sauce.

Season with a little salt, plenty of pepper and a little grated Parmesan to taste.

Perfect Eggs on Toast

When it's all too much, when I'm in a hurry, when I just don't know what in the world it is that I want to eat, I make scrambled eggs and I eat them on hot, buttered toast. I cook the eggs the way my mother makes them (likewise, when she's in a hurry, hungry and it's all too much): just eggs and butter cooked gently over the lowest possible heat, stirring constantly ('whatever you do, don't stop stirring!'). Her method gives you a scramble that is somewhere between butter, cream and a broken omelet: a sunny, soothing mush. Her trick is to take the eggs off the heat just before you think they're done, so they're still soft – to the point of almost being runny – rather than dry; but if you prefer your eggs more solid, then of course just cook them for a short while longer. This is fast food, but it also happens to be soul-soothing food.

For me, just the eggs on toast is pretty much a perfect meal in itself, be it for breakfast, lunch or dinner, perhaps with the addition of a thin scraping of Marmite on the toast or a hefty grinding of pepper over the eggs, depending on my mood and the time of day. But you can of course bulk the eggs out with something more: slices of smoked salmon, a little spinach on the side (just the frozen kind, pan-fried until thawed and warmed through, then dressed with some butter and salt), a light green salad, sliced tomatoes, half an avocado served with a drizzle of olive oil and a smattering of red pepper flakes, or slices of paper-thin, salty prosciutto.

Any which way, I'm always happy to eat this, as is the rest of my family... which in itself is often half the battle.

This recipe contains lightly cooked eggs, so take all the usual precautions, if you need to do so (see page 70).

HANDS ON TIME:
10 minutes
SERVES 4

12 eggs
3 tbsp salted butter, plus
    more for the toast
4 thick slices of bread
freshly ground
    black pepper

Crack the eggs into a medium-sized saucepan and beat lightly with a fork. Add the butter and a couple of grindings of black pepper and set the pan over a very low heat.

Put your bread on to toast.

Stir the eggs constantly with a wooden spoon, and, as they cook, scrape the bottom of the pan every now and then to incorporate the more solid bits into the liquid. After 5–6 minutes, the eggs should be scrambled but still runny, a little like the texture of sloppy oatmeal. If you like your eggs fluffy rather than soft and mushy, then leave the pan over the heat a little while longer.

Take the pan off the heat and keep stirring: remember that the eggs will keep on cooking from the heat of the pan and will continue to solidify.

Arrange the toast on plates, slather in butter, then tip the soft scrambled eggs over each slice. Season with a little more pepper to taste and serve immediately.

Red Bell Pepper and Feta Frittata

Wrapped in parchment paper, this will keep for two or three days in the fridge, then serve at room temperature. Especially good fare for picnics, just slice it up before you go.

Frittata always feels like a good solution for dinner, because all you need to make it is what you already have in the kitchen (pretty much whatever that is will do), plus eggs. It's one of those dishes that has a hash-like quality about it; and the recipe below should provide a template for you to make your own with whatever it is you have to play with. I'll happily throw in leftover roasted or boiled potatoes, onion, any kind (or, indeed, many kinds) of cheese, olives, herbs, spinach, zucchini, broccoli, beans, asparagus – raw or cooked – pancetta, chorizo, tomatoes, you name it... But on those days when I do have the forethought to plan dinner and to think about exactly what kind of frittata I might want to cook us all, then this particular combination – tender, sweet peppers, almost caramelized in the pan, with a crumbling of snowy white, blunt and exquisitely salty feta – is perhaps my favorite. I like to finish my frittata off in the oven, which I find gives it a nice golden glow all over, so I make it in a pan with an ovenproof handle. If you don't have one, you can either turn the frittata out on to a roasting pan and put that in the oven (though that does involve more dishwashing than seems sensible for a simple dish), or cover the pan and finish cooking the frittata on the stove. You won't get that golden color on the top as well as the bottom, but it will still taste every bit as good.

HANDS ON TIME:
15 minutes

HANDS OFF TIME:
15 minutes on the stove;
10–15 minutes in the oven

SERVES 6

2 tbsp olive oil

1 onion, chopped

1 red bell pepper, sliced
   into ½-inch-thick strips

7 tbsp water

9 eggs

scant ½ cup grated
   Parmesan cheese

leaves from a small bunch
   of parsley, chopped

1 cup crumbled feta cheese

Heat the oil over a medium-high heat in a large ovenproof frying pan. Add the onion and bell pepper and fry gently for 3–5 minutes until slightly colored, then reduce the heat a little, add the measured water and cook for 10–12 minutes until the liquid has evaporated and the pepper has softened a little.

Crack the eggs into a bowl and lightly beat with a fork. Add the Parmesan and beat lightly again to combine.

Once the pepper is cooked, sprinkle over the parsley and feta and pour in the eggs. Reduce the heat to low and cook gently on the stove for 15 minutes, until the bottom of the frittata is set and lightly colored. Meanwhile, heat the oven to 350°F.

Now put the frittata in the oven to cook for a further 10–15 minutes or so, until the top has set and is lightly colored. Serve warm or at room temperature.

Tomato, Mozzarella and Black Olive Tart

🎁 *Package up in a cake box or airtight container. It keeps happily in the fridge for up to two days.*

I first made this tart for a summer picnic, to eat barefoot on the grass under the dappled shade of the big chestnut tree on the Common where we always go to picnic as soon as the days feel warm enough. And that's how I'll always think of it: sun-drenched, and the kind of happy food you can eat with your fingers.

This tart has all the classic, crowd-pleasing flavors, which is why it's consistently a winner at home: mild, melted mozzarella, cherry tomatoes (barely cooked so you can really taste them, little explosions of sweet juices with every bite) and moreish olives, which the boys and I adore. But you should also play around with the recipe as you please: think perhaps of adding some salty capers, anchovies for those (like me) who love them, chunks of zucchini or slices of fennel if you want to get more greens in there, or shavings of hard, punchier cheese such as pecorino or Parmesan in place of – or in addition to – the grated Cheddar. You could even fry up a little pancetta along with the onion and throw it in there too.

Whatever and whichever way you make it, this is one of those dishes that's always a joy to eat.

HANDS ON TIME:
20 minutes
HANDS OFF TIME:
40–55 minutes in the oven
SERVES 6

3 ⅓ cups cherry or grape
  tomatoes
5 tbsp olive oil
½ tsp dried oregano
10oz fresh mozzarella
  cheese, chopped
1 store-bought refrigerated
  pie crust (from a 14.1-oz
  package)
1 small red onion,
  finely chopped
scant 1½ cups grated mild
  Cheddar cheese
handful of pitted black
  olives, preferably
  Taggiasche
leaves from a small bunch
  of basil
leaves from a small bunch
  of mint
flaky sea salt and freshly
  ground black pepper

Heat the oven to 400°F.

Throw the cherry tomatoes whole into a small bowl, drizzle with 3 tbsp olive oil, a generous pinch of salt, a good grind of pepper and the sprinkle of dried oregano, then leave to marinate for a while. Set the chopped mozzarella in a colander to drain excess liquid.

Drape the pie crust over a 10-inch loose-bottomed fluted tart pan and press it into the pan. Pierce the base all over with a fork, then cover with a sheet of parchment paper and fill with baking beans. Blind-bake in the oven for 10–15 minutes, until the tart crust is golden at the edges. Remove the beans and bake for a further 10 minutes until dry to the touch.

Heat the remaining 2 tbsp olive oil in a medium-sized frying pan, then add the onion along with a generous pinch of salt. Fry over a medium heat for 3–5 minutes, until the onion turns soft and translucent, then remove from the heat.

Take the tart pan out of the oven and reduce the oven temperature to 350°F. Spoon the onion evenly all over the tart crust. Scatter two-thirds of the mozzarella and half the Cheddar over, then arrange the whole tomatoes in there snugly, draining away any excess liquid. Scatter the oily black olives in among the tomatoes and dot a few basil and mint leaves around them, then top with the last of the cheese: mozzarella first and then a sprinkle of the grated Cheddar on top of that.

Return the tart to the oven and bake for a further 20–30 minutes, until the cheese is melted and golden.

Bread Pizza

⊞ *Wrapped in parchment paper, this will keep for one or two days in the fridge. Just gently reheat in the oven before serving.*

This really should be 'pizza' rather than pizza, as it resembles something more of the deep-base, Chicago-style variety than Neapolitan pizza in any authentic sense. The base is stale bread, softened in olive oil and baked in a cake pan to make a thick pillowy base for your choice of topping. Perhaps not the most refined dish, but all the more delicious for that: the boys and I both adore it and it's great fun to make. With a thin-based pizza, I tend to prefer a 'white' (tomato-free) topping: just cheese and prosciutto, or wilted greens, or thick chunks of spicy salame; but this kind of pizza needs that dollop of the tomato sauce to top it – the umami-filled juices seep into the top layer of the bread base infusing it with flavor – and heaps of melted mozzarella. As to what else to put on top, think of it as a blank canvas: I love salty anchovies because of the punch of flavor, and green olives, very much for the same reason. But you could add grilled vegetables (bell peppers, sliced zucchini and so on). I've always had a soft spot for pineapple and ham on pizza, as outrageous as this might seem, otherwise you could go for something classic such as ham, baby artichokes (the kind that come in a jar) and olives.

HANDS ON TIME:
10 minutes

HANDS OFF TIME:
25–30 minutes in the oven

SERVES 4

⅓ cup olive oil, plus more
   for the pan
10oz (about 10 medium
   slices) stale crusty bread
½ cup plus 1 tbsp cold
   water
scant 1 cup tomato passata,
   or good-quality tomato
   sauce
8oz fresh mozzarella
   cheese, sliced
3 anchovies
handful of pitted olives
leaves from a few
   basil sprigs

Heat the oven to 350°F. Oil a 9-inch springform cake pan and line it with parchment paper.

Tear the bread into ¾-inch chunks. Toss the bread in a mixing bowl, pour over the measured water, little by little, to soften the bread, then pour over the olive oil to give it flavor. Mix everything together with your hands to make sure all the chunks of bread are well coated.

Press the soaked bread into the prepared pan. Spoon the tomato passata over the base, spreading it right to the edges of the pan.

Top with the slices of milky-white mozzarella, then dot the anchovies, olives and basil leaves here and there.

Bake in the oven for 25–30 minutes, until the cheese is completely melted, and when you insert a knife to the middle it feels warm to the touch.

Honey Roasted Chicken Thighs with Golden Potatoes

This is a put-it-all-in-one-roasting-pan-and-shove-it-in-the-oven kind of a dish, guaranteed to delight grown-ups and little ones alike. You could just chop the potatoes very small and toss them in the roasting pan as is, but if at all possible I do prefer to go to the bother of par-boiling them first (albeit not of peeling them), then dusting in a spoonful of flour before tossing them in the roasting pan. Because – and trust me when I say this – this method gives you the most exquisitely golden and crisp roasted potatoes, and, on balance, while it does leave you with an extra pan to wash, it's neither a complicated nor particularly time-consuming business, I think it is very much worth it. I smear the chicken skin in a honeyed marinade that not only infuses the tender meat with flavor, but the potatoes too. The quantities below are a guide for when I cook this at home for two adults and two children, so while I suggest that it serves four, if you're cooking for four hungry adults you may want to increase the quantities of potatoes and, indeed, chicken thighs: to do this, the method stays the same, but you'll likely need a second roasting pan to fit everything in.

HANDS ON TIME:
15 minutes
HANDS OFF TIME:
55 minutes in the oven
SERVES 4

1¼lbs potatoes
1 tbsp all-purpose flour
5 tbsp olive oil
4–6 skin-on bone-in
   chicken thighs
1 tbsp honey
flaky sea salt and freshly
   ground black pepper

Heat the oven to 400°F.

Chop the potatoes into roughly 1-inch chunks, toss them into a saucepan, cover with cold water and add a generous pinch of salt. Bring to a boil over a medium heat, then cook for 8–10 minutes. Drain in a colander.

Rough the potatoes up in the colander, then toss them into a roasting pan. Sprinkle over the flour and shake until they're all evenly coated. Drizzle over ¼ cup olive oil and set in the oven to roast for 20 minutes, taking care to spread the potatoes out well in the pan so they become nice and golden.

After 20 minutes or so, turn the potatoes and add the chicken thighs to the roasting pan. Combine the honey and the remaining 1 tbsp olive oil together in a small bowl, whisk lightly with a fork to combine, then drizzle liberally over the chicken. Sprinkle with salt and pepper.

Put the pan back in the oven and roast for a further 35 minutes, until the chicken skin turns golden and crisp and the juices run clear when you insert a knife into the thickest part of a thigh.

Eat with some kind of green vegetable, perhaps the Golden Crisp Leeks (see page 182), or anything else you fancy.

Polpette alla Ricotta
with Tomato Sauce

✾ *Store the polpette swimming in their tomato sauce in an airtight container in the fridge for one or two days, then warm them through in a saucepan as per the recipe (make sure to include cooking instructions).*

The thing to remember here is to drain the ricotta in advance: you can do this overnight or even just for a couple of hours before you start cooking, but you absolutely mustn't skip this step as it will ensure the ricotta balls hold their shape nicely and don't turn soggy or collapse in the pan.

For the rest, you can let your children loose to make these: making the mixture and rolling it into small balls. It's hours of entertainment and this is one of those recipes you can't really go wrong with: more cheese, more nutmeg, no nutmeg, you name it. I've eaten every version of it and it has always been a delight.

I tend to take over when it comes to cooking the polpette in the tomato sauce, just because there are hot pans and hot bubbling liquid involved, but the boys always like to watch next to me just to check I'm doing it right, then we all enjoy eating this for dinner with a good loaf of crusty bread to mop up the tomato juices, and perhaps a dish of something simple and green, such as spinach with a little butter, a crisp green salad or the fava beans dressed with feta and toasted almonds at page 181.

HANDS ON TIME:
30 minutes
HANDS OFF TIME:
2 hours, or up to overnight,
to drain the ricotta
SERVES 4

scant 1½ cups ricotta
5oz stale white bread,
    crusts removed
1 tsp freshly grated nutmeg
2 large eggs
1 cup grated Parmesan
    cheese, plus more
    to serve
2 tbsp olive oil
1 garlic clove, peeled
scant 3 cups tomato sauce
handful of basil leaves,
    plus more to serve
flaky sea salt and freshly
    ground black pepper

Spoon the ricotta into a strainer, set it over a bowl and leave it in the fridge for a couple of hours (or overnight) to drain as much of the excess liquid as possible.

Blitz the stale bread in a food processor to make coarse breadcrumbs; no need for refinement here. You should have about 2 heaping cups.

In a large mixing bowl, combine the drained ricotta and crumbs. Add the nutmeg and stir it in. Lightly beat the eggs with a fork in a second small bowl, then add them to the ricotta. Add the Parmesan and use a fork to bring the ingredients together into something that resembles soft modeling clay. Season to taste with salt and pepper.

Scoop a little mixture into your hands, roll it into a ball roughly the size of a golf ball, then set on a clean plate or baking sheet. The mixture should give you 16–18 balls.

Heat the olive oil in a large frying pan over a medium heat, add the whole garlic clove and fry it gently for 4–5 minutes until browned all over and the oil is infused with its flavor. Remove the garlic and discard.

Take the pan off the heat, add the tomato sauce, then set the pan back over the heat. Add the basil leaves, season with a little pepper and bring to a gentle simmer.

Carefully lower the ricotta balls into the sauce, distributing them evenly in the pan. Simmer gently for 10 minutes or so, then turn the balls over in the sauce and let them cook on the other side for a further 5 minutes.

To test if they are cooked through, slice one open and touch the center with your finger: it should feel warm right the way through. Spoon the last of the tomato sauce over the polpette, then dot with a few more basil leaves and a dash of grated Parmesan before eating.

Tonno alla Filicudara

The first time we ate tuna cooked this way, swimming in a tomato sauce peppered with olives and capers, was on holiday in the remote island of Filicudi in the Aeolian Islands off the coast of Sicily. It tastes like sunshine and summer days even when you cook it at home. Even – and especially – when it's cold, dark and raining.

HANDS ON TIME:
25 minutes
SERVES 4

2 tbsp olive oil
1 red onion, thinly sliced
4 cups cherry or grape
    tomatoes, halved
2 tbsp capers
heaping ½ cup pitted black
    olives
leaves from a small bunch
    of mint, chopped
4 small tuna steaks
flaky sea salt and freshly
    ground black pepper

Heat the oil in a large frying pan over a medium heat. Add the onion and a generous pinch of salt. Cook for 10–15 minutes, until softened and translucent.

Throw the tomatoes into the pan, along with the capers, olives and mint. Cook everything together, stirring now and then with a spoon, for 3–5 minutes, until the tomatoes begin to soften and release their juices. Season to taste with salt and pepper.

Gently arrange the tuna steaks in the pan in between the tomatoes and cook for 1–2 minutes on each side for rare, or 2–3 minutes on each side for cooked through.

Pollo alla Pizzaiola

While chicken breast is undoubtedly an easy, quick and uncontroversial option for dinner, I find it often to be quite disappointing: a little bland, usually dry and just a bit boring. Except when cooked this way: the meat is browned, then lightly poached in rich tomato sauce so it stays exquisitely tender, and each piece comes enrobed in a blanket of melting mozzarella cheese. Absolutely essential with this is some crusty bread for wiping up all the juices on your plate. And depending on your mood, you might also want a light salad or a few greens.

HANDS ON TIME:
20 minutes
SERVES 4

2 tbsp olive oil
4 skinless, boneless
 chicken breasts
scant 2 cups good-quality
 tomato sauce
2-3 tbsp capers
leaves from a small bunch
 of basil, chopped
8oz fresh mozzarella
 cheese, sliced
flaky sea salt and freshly
 ground black pepper

Heat the olive oil in a large frying pan that has a lid; you want a pan that is large enough to fit the 4 chicken breasts. Brown the meat on both sides over a medium heat, then take the pan off the heat. Take the breasts out of the pan, set on a plate and season them generously with salt and pepper.

Put the tomato sauce in the frying pan while the pan is still off the heat, so the difference in temperature between sauce and hot pan doesn't cause the sauce to spit, then put the pan back over the heat to warm through. Add the capers and basil. When the tomato begins to bubble, nestle the seasoned chicken in the pan.

Cook the chicken in the pan over a medium heat for 7-8 minutes, turning the breasts every now and then, until cooked through.

Lay a slice or 2 of mozzarella over each piece of chicken and cover the pan with its lid, or, if you don't have a lid big enough, you can cover the pan with foil. Cook for a further minute or 2, until the cheese is melted. Serve immediately.

Effortless Melanzane alla Parmigiana

⊞ Cook this in a baking dish, then cover with foil and drop off with instructions to reheat covered, in a medium oven, until warm in the center. It will keep in the fridge for two or three days and freezes like a dream.

A great classic of Italian cooking, crowd-pleasing and rousing in the same way as that aria in a Puccini opera everyone intuitively somehow knows the rhythm of in their hearts: it is certainly one of my favorite things to eat. The layers of melted cheese, the soupy tomato sauce and the tender eggplant, all together it makes for the most delightfully comforting combination, and needs little to go with it; some buttered wilted spinach on the side, perhaps, or a crisp green salad, or a big spoonful of fava beans dressed with crumbled feta and sliced almonds (see page 181).

Traditionally, you deep-fry the slices of eggplant before layering them with cheese and tomato, but here I skip that step. In part this is for sheer ease: done this way, the business of making the *melanzane alla Parmigiana* is more a matter of assembly, not so much of actual cooking, and the boys therefore can meaningfully help me with it. I also, however, find that I prefer it this way: it makes for a lighter, less oily dish; the eggplant, just lightly poached from the heat of the sauce it comes swimming in, holds a firmer, drier texture and an almost meaty flavor that I really enjoy.

I use bottled tomato passata for this – the very best kind I can find in the store – then season generously with basil leaves and a dash of good olive oil: I find this works beautifully and saves on time, but you could of course make your own tomato sauce if you prefer and have a treasured recipe, or use the recipe for tomato sauce in Pasta alla Bibi (see page 148) for a more rustic affair.

HANDS ON TIME:

15 minutes

HANDS OFF TIME:

60–65 minutes in the oven;
15 minutes resting

SERVES 4

1 very large (or 2 small)
   eggplant(s), total weight
   about 14oz

2 cups tomato passata, or
   good-quality tomato
   sauce

large handful of basil
   leaves

2 tbsp olive oil

14oz fresh mozzarella
   cheese, sliced

heaping ¾ cup grated
   Parmesan cheese

flaky sea salt and freshly
   ground black pepper

Heat the oven to 375°F.

Slice the eggplant(s) lengthways into pieces roughly ½ inch thick. Throw the slices into a 13 x 9-inch ovenproof dish (the same one in which you will cook the Parmigiana), ideally in a single layer, and bake for 15–20 minutes, until the eggplant is very lightly colored and feels spongy and tender to the touch.

Take the dish out of the oven and set the eggplant to one side.

Spoon half the tomato passata into the dish. Roughly tear a few basil leaves and sprinkle them over the sauce, drizzle over 1 tbsp olive oil and season generously with salt and pepper.

Arrange half the eggplant slices over the tomato so they sit snugly in the dish and top with half the mozzarella and half the Parmesan. Spoon over the last of the tomato passata, drizzle with a second tbsp of oil and toss in a few more torn basil leaves. Arrange the last of the eggplant slices in a second layer and top with the remaining mozzarella and a few more basil leaves.

Sprinkle the rest of the Parmesan over the top of the dish and bake in the oven for 45 minutes, until warmed through and the cheese is melted and golden on top. To test if it's cooked, insert a knife to the middle of the dish: if the blade comes out warm to the touch, it's done. Let rest for 15 minutes, then serve while still piping hot.

Fava Beans with Feta and Almonds

⌘ *Store in an airtight container in the fridge for one or two days. Serve at room temperature. This is another dish that is great for picnics.*

I always keep a bag or two of fava beans in my freezer, largely so that when I find myself improvising supper, looking for some kind of vegetable to go with steak or leftover roast chicken or whatever it is, I can make this dish. It's simplicity itself: you boil the beans for a couple of minutes and then top with a smattering of salty, snowy-white feta cheese and golden, toasted sliced almonds. You can play with the beans as you like: dress them simply with a glug of olive oil and a smattering of mint leaves, if you have them to hand, crumble over some toasted breadcrumbs if you like (a great way to use up stale bread), or grate in the zest of a lemon and add a generous squeeze of lemon juice along with the olive oil; the acidity is a lovely, zingy complement to the buttery beans. These are every bit as delightful served at room temperature as they are still hot and steaming from the pan.

HANDS ON TIME:
10 minutes
SERVES 4-6

½ tbsp salted butter

heaping ⅓ cup sliced
   almonds

4 cups frozen, shelled fava
   or edamame beans

2-3 tbsp olive oil

leaves from a small bunch
   of mint, chopped

heaping ¾ cup crumbled
   feta cheese

flaky sea salt

Melt the butter in a small frying pan over a medium heat, then add ½ tsp salt and the sliced almonds. Fry for 2–3 minutes, shaking from time to time, until the almonds are golden brown. Take the pan off the heat and set to one side.

Bring a large saucepan of water to a boil and salt generously. When the water begins to gallop, add the frozen beans and cook for 3–5 minutes. Drain well, then toss the beans back in the pan. Dress with 2 tbsp olive oil and salt to taste (remember that the feta cheese is quite salty, so err on the side of caution here).

Toss the beans with the mint, then put into a serving dish. Scatter over the feta and the toasted almonds and dress with one last glug of olive oil, if you like. Serve warm or at room temperature.

Golden Crisp Leeks

Barely a Sunday supper passes by when I don't roast a pan or two of leeks this way: slowly, slowly, on a low heat, until they become almost melt-in-your-mouth tender, then at the last hurdle, I crank the oven up high so the outer leaves crisp and turn golden brown. It's like eating potato chips, but better. It may seem like an outrageously generous amount of olive oil, and an improbably long cooking time, but trust me on both: the results are well worth it.

HANDS ON TIME:
5 minutes
HANDS OFF TIME:
1¾ hours in the oven
SERVES 4

3 leeks
⅓ cup olive oil
flaky sea salt and freshly
   ground black pepper

Heat the oven to 325°F.

Trim the leeks and run them under cold water to wash away any grit or dirt that may be caught in between the leaves. Slice the leeks in half, from top to tail, and arrange them snugly, side by side, in a roasting pan.

Drizzle over the olive oil and season generously with salt and pepper. Cover the dish with foil and set to bake in the oven for 1½ hours. The leeks should be cooked through and softened by this point.

Now, remove the foil, increase the oven temperature to 375°F and roast the leeks for a further 10–15 minutes, until the outer leaves are deliciously golden and crisp.

Sugared Plum Pudding

🎁 *Cook this in a baking dish, then cover with reusable food wrap and drop off with instructions to reheat in a medium oven until warmed through. You might want to add a pot of heavy cream to the bundle, too.*

The recipe below is barely adapted from the recipe for plum-topped bread pudding in Jocasta Innes's timelessly brilliant *The Pauper's Cookbook*: my only variations to Innes's *chef-d'oeuvre* are fresh fruit rather than canned, and brioche rather than stale white or brown bread. This is largely because I have a soft spot for the pillowy sweetness of brioche and the way the edges of it crisp ever so slightly as the pudding bakes in the oven while the middle stays cloud-like soft, but you could of course make this with any bread you like. You could also play around with the fruit: when in season, use sweet apricots (and perhaps in that case substitute chopped pistachios for the flaked almonds), wedges of sweet nectarine or white peach in high summer. In the winter, I quite often tip a bag of frozen mixed summer berries over the layer of thick buttered bread. All in all, this is sheer, delectable comfort to eat. I can happily delegate the buttering of sliced brioche to my boys; it keeps them entertained for a good while (though I would allow for extra bread and butter as a fair amount goes missing in the making of the pudding).

HANDS ON TIME:
15 minutes
HANDS OFF TIME:
35–40 minutes in the oven
SERVES 6

12oz stale brioche,
  or challah
6 tbsp salted butter
heaping ¼ cup sliced
  almonds
2 tsp ground cinnamon
1¾lbs plums
½ cup turbinado sugar
crème anglaise, ice cream
  or lightly whipped
  cream, to serve
  (optional)

Heat the oven to 350°F.

Slice the brioche into 1-inch thick slices and butter generously on both sides. Lay the buttered bread into a 13 x 9-inch ovenproof dish that is about 2½ inches deep, pressing the slices snugly together so the dish is completely covered. Sprinkle the sliced almonds and 1 tsp cinnamon over the bread.

Halve the plums and discard the pits. Press the fruit, cut side up, firmly into the bread and again arrange snugly together so the dish is filled with fruit.

In a small bowl, combine the sugar and the last of the cinnamon, stir to mix well, then sprinkle over the plums.

Bake in the oven for 35–40 minutes until the plum juices begin to bubble and run, and when you insert a butter knife to a plum you feel no resistance.

Serve warm straight from the oven with a goodly dollop of crème anglaise, ice cream or whipped cream, as you please.

Baked Ricotta al Limone

🎁 *This will keep happily in the fridge (or even in a cool room) for three or four days. Store in a cake box or large airtight container.*

I never used to like lemon-flavored desserts until I had this. It's a cheesecake of sorts, but pudding-like. It's not sickly sweet as I find so many lemon desserts are, but mellow and gentle in flavor with just a hint of fresh citrus. You can bake it in a cake pan or a mold, as you please; we bake ours in an old copper gelatin mold shaped like a large daisy and the result tastes and looks like sunshine.

HANDS ON TIME:
10 minutes
HANDS OFF TIME:
60–70 minutes in the oven
SERVES 8-10

salted butter, for the pan
2 tbsp all-purpose flour, for
  the pan
4 eggs
3 cups ricotta
1¾ cups confectioners'
  sugar
5 tbsp lemon juice
7 tbsp heavy cream
1 cup cornstarch

Heat the oven to 325°F. Butter a 9-inch cake pan, or the equivalent-sized mold, and dust down with the flour, tipping the pan or mold to evenly coat it all over. Shake out any excess flour.

Separate the eggs. In a large mixing bowl, combine the yolks, ricotta and confectioners' sugar and beat until smooth. Add the lemon juice and beat again just to combine, then beat in the cream. Lastly add the cornstarch and, again, beat until smooth.

In a second, spotlessly clean mixing bowl, whisk the egg whites until they are stiff. Fold them into the lemony batter, then pour it into the prepared pan or mold.

Bake for 60–70 minutes, until lightly golden and firm to the touch. If it is browning too much, then cover with foil and continue to bake until set.

Let cool in the pan, then turn out on to a serving dish.

Sweet Potato and Marshmallow Pie

✤ *This really tastes best on the day of baking, or the next day. Ideally bake it in a foil pie dish and package in a cake box with instructions to reheat in a medium oven.*

Thanksgiving isn't a holiday that I grew up with; it's one I've adopted along the way. And it's not a dissimilar story for this pie: I first made it in honor of American friends round about the holidays. We were improvising a 'friendsgiving' with roast chicken rather than turkey (it's hard to get your hands on a turkey in Britain in the weeks outside Christmas) and I wanted to make something with some semblance of authenticity, the kind of food I have seen in movies and read about in books. And so I made this, and found myself so deeply seduced by the flavors – the warmth of the spiced sweet potato and the sweet chewiness of the caramelized marshmallow topping – that we've adopted it into our family repertoire of winter favorites. And perhaps because I didn't grow up with Thanksgiving but have come to adopt it (and this pie), I am unencumbered by tradition and happily bake and eat this all through winter.

HANDS ON TIME:
15–20 minutes
HANDS OFF TIME:
1 hour 30 minutes–1 hour
35 minutes in the oven
SERVES 8-10

5 medium-sized sweet
    potatoes (total weight
    about 2¼lbs)
1 tsp olive oil
3 tbsp salted butter
2 tsp ground cinnamon
1 store-bought refrigerated
    pie crust (from a 14.1-oz
    package)
30–32 regular-sized
    marshmallows

Heat the oven to 400°F.

Prick the sweet potatoes with a fork, rub each with olive oil and wrap individually in foil. Roast for 1 hour, until you can insert a fork to the potatoes and feel little resistance. Now reduce the oven temperature to 350°F.

When they are cool enough to handle, scoop the flesh out of the potatoes and discard the skins. Combine the sweet potatoes, butter and cinnamon together in a mixing bowl and mash until smooth.

Drape the pie crust over a 10-inch loose-bottomed tart pan and press it in. Trim away and discard any excess and prick the base all over with a fork. Cover with parchment paper and fill the tart crust with baking beans, then blind-bake in the oven for 15 minutes until the pastry starts to color at the edges. Remove the parchment and the beans, then bake for a further 5 minutes, until the base feels dry to the touch.

Spoon the mashed sweet potato into the tart crust and spread it out evenly with the back of the spoon. Top with the marshmallows, leaving a little space between each one and a ½-inch gap around the edge, then bake in the oven for 10–15 minutes, until melted and lightly golden on top.

Rhubarb and Almond Cake

🎁 *Package up in a cake box or airtight container. It will keep for two to three days.*

The idea to throw chopped rhubarb into cake batter, raw, like little sticks of pink Brighton rock candy, comes to me via my friend Sarah Standing, veritable domestic goddess and architect of the date and rosemary-studded soda bread (see page 240) as well as the honeyed apricot and walnut salad (see page 269), both of which are such staples in my kitchen. It is sheer genius. I've taken a version of the River Café's inimitable recipe for polenta cake as my base, which is equal parts buttery and crumbly and a pleasing golden yellow hue, and through it you get shards of sour rhubarb, pops of intense pink color and flavor. By the same principle, you could throw some raspberries (frozen or fresh), blackberries or even blueberries in there. Though candy-pink rhubarb, when in season, will always have my heart. And this is a hearty cake.

HANDS ON TIME:
10 minutes
HANDS OFF TIME:
1 hour 10 minutes–1 hour 15 minutes in the oven
SERVES 10

3 sticks plus 1 tbsp (370g) salted butter, softened, plus more for the pan
1¾ cups plus 1 tbsp (370g) superfine sugar
3¾ cups (370g) almond meal
2 tsp vanilla extract
5 eggs
3 tbsp milk
1 cup plus 2 tbsp (190g) polenta
1½ tsp baking powder
3–4 skinny stalks (approximately 10oz) rhubarb, chopped into 1-inch pieces (about 3 cups)
flaky sea salt

Heat the oven to 375°F. Butter a 9-inch springform cake pan and line it with parchment paper.

Beat the butter and sugar together until pale and light. Stir in the almond meal and vanilla. Now beat in the eggs, one at a time, followed by the milk. Lastly, fold in the polenta, baking powder and ½ tsp salt.

Spoon the batter into the prepared cake pan, then drop in the chunks of rhubarb, scattering them evenly though the cake.

Bake in the oven for 1 hour 10 minutes–1 hour 15 minutes, until the cake is set and brown on top. Let cool in the pan, then turn the cake out on to a dish or stand.

Orange Loaf Cake

⊞ *Packaged up in a cake box or airtight container, this will keep for two or three days.*

There are moments in life when only a loaf cake will do: when you want something sweet, but not too sweet; when you crave the soothing comfort of plain not-quite-bread-not-quite-cake cake. This loaf cake, dense with almonds, mellow flavored, lightly spiced and softly scented with the juice and zest of an orange, is for just those moments. And misguidedly perhaps, because it doesn't come layered with buttercream or rolled fondant icing, because it looks like a plain cake, it's something I'll happily let the boys help themselves to at will.

HANDS ON TIME:
10 minutes
HANDS OFF TIME:
30–35 minutes in the oven
SERVES 6-8

butter, for the pan
3 eggs
½ cup plus 1 tbsp superfine
   sugar
finely grated zest and juice
   of 1 orange
¾ cup plus 2 tbsp (100g)
   all-purpose flour
1½ tsp baking powder
1 cup (100g) almond meal
½ tsp ground cinnamon
½ tsp ground ginger
flaky sea salt
confectioners' sugar,
   to dust

Heat the oven to 350°F. Butter a 2lb-capacity loaf pan, then line it with parchment paper.

Separate the eggs. Combine the yolks in a large mixing bowl with the sugar and whisk until they turn a light, lemony color. Now add the orange zest and juice and whisk together until well combined. Add the flour, baking powder, almond meal, spices and a generous pinch of salt and stir with a wooden spoon until well combined.

In a second, spotlessly clean bowl, whisk the egg whites until they look like fluffy clouds, then fold them into the cake batter, trying to keep as much of the air in there as possible.

Pour the batter into the prepared pan and set in the oven for 30–35 minutes, until a knife comes out clean when inserted to the middle. Let the cake cool in the pan for 5 minutes for so, then turn it out on to a wire rack to cool completely.

Dust with confectioners' sugar before serving.

Birthday Cake of Dreams

🎁 *Carefully package in a cake box. This cake will keep well for two or three days in a cool room (or store in the fridge if it's especially warm weather).*

I first made a version of this for Aeneas's birthday a few years ago, and it has, with time, evolved into this magnificently indulgent beast. What makes it so special is the pockets of runny chocolate. For the frosting, I've adapted Mary Henderson's 'Nanny's Icing' and I can't tell you how unbelievably good it tastes. As the frosting contains raw eggs, take all the usual precautions, if you need to do so (see page 70).

HANDS ON TIME:
35 minutes
HANDS OFF TIME:
65–75 minutes in the oven;
SERVES 12

FOR THE CAKE
3 sticks plus 3 tbsp salted
    butter, softened
2½ cups (600g) chocolate-
    hazelnut spread
2 cups (400g) superfine
    sugar
1 cup (240g) plain whole
    milk yogurt
6 eggs
3 cups plus 2 tbsp (400g)
    all-purpose flour
5¼ tsp baking powder
¾ cup (80g) unsweetened
    cocoa powder

FOR THE FROSTING
2 sticks (240g) salted
    butter, softened
4 ⅓ cups (440g)
    confectioners' sugar
4 egg yolks
1⅔ cups (400g) chocolate-
    hazelnut spread
3–4 tbsp milk
nonpareils, to decorate

Heat the oven to 350°F. Butter two 9-inch springform cake pans and line them with parchment paper.

Spoon a heaping ¾ cup (200g) chocolate-hazelnut spread into an ice cube tray, using roughly 1 heaping tsp in each cavity, then set in the freezer for 10 minutes or so, until the cubes feel solid.

In a large mixing bowl, beat the butter, remaining scant 1¾ cups (400g) chocolate-hazelnut spread and superfine sugar until combined. Slowly beat in the yogurt and eggs. Sift in the flour, baking powder and cocoa powder, a spoonful at a time and beating all the while, until you have a smooth batter. Divide it equally between the 2 pans.

Take the chocolate-hazelnut cubes out of the freezer and nestle them in towards the center of the 2 cakes, so that they're completely concealed in cake batter.

Bake the cakes in the oven for 35–40 minutes, then cover with foil and bake for a further 30–35 minutes, until the tops of the cakes spring back when you press down on them gently with your fingers and a knife comes out clean when inserted to the middle. Leave the cakes to cool for 10 minutes or so in their pans, then turn them out and let cool completely on a wire rack.

To make the frosting, beat the butter with an electric mixer until soft and light. In a second bowl, beat the confectioners' sugar and egg yolks together until well combined, then add the butter and beat until smooth. Add the chocolate-hazelnut spread and beat until combined. Lastly add the milk and beat again until smooth.

Spoon a generous dollop of the frosting over the first chocolate cake and spread out evenly. Sandwich together with the second cake and frost all over the top and sides. Decorate with nonpareils and birthday candles.

Berry Crumble Cake

🎁 *Packaged up in a cake box or airtight container, this will keep well for three days.*

Perhaps not the prettiest of cakes: topped as it is with a messy rubble of turbinado sugar, butter and crumbled amaretti cookies, its appearance is one of humble brownness rather than anything showy. Nonetheless my son Aeneas claims that he prefers this to chocolate and I must say I almost agree. It's halfway between a sharp, jammy berry crumble and a dense vanilla sponge cake. When in season, you could of course make it with fresh berries, but frozen works just as well and, I must admit, for sheer ease, does tend to be my default.

HANDS ON TIME:
10–15 minutes
HANDS OFF TIME:
40–45 minutes in the oven, plus cooling
SERVES 8

FOR THE CRUMBLE
1 stick (110g) salted butter, softened
5 tbsp (50g) all-purpose flour
2 tbsp (30g) each turbinado sugar and superfine sugar
4oz (100g) amaretti cookies

FOR THE CAKE
1 stick (120g) salted butter, softened
½ cup (100g) superfine sugar
2 eggs
1 tsp vanilla extract
1⅔ cups (200g) all-purpose flour
2¾ tsp baking powder
7 tbsp (100ml) whole milk
2½ cups (250g) mixed frozen berries
flaky sea salt

Heat the oven to 350°F. Butter a 9-inch springform cake pan and line it with parchment paper.

Begin by making the crumble topping: combine the flour and sugars together in a medium-sized bowl, then rub in the butter. Crumble in the amaretti cookies (about 2 cups) and again rub together with your fingers until you have a lumpy crumble. Set to one side.

For the cake, beat the butter and sugar together until light and fluffy, then add the eggs one at a time and beat until well combined. Beat in the vanilla, then sift in half the flour and a pinch of salt and beat until smooth. Now add the milk, sift in the remaining flour and stir with a wooden spoon until just combined.

Spoon the batter into the cake pan and smooth out. Sprinkle the berries over the batter in a single layer. Crumble the amaretti topping over the cake, covering the berries completely.

Bake for 40–45 minutes, until a knife comes out clean when inserted to the middle. Leave to cool in the pan until barely warm, then slide out on to a plate.

Chocolate Chunk Bundt Cake

🎁 *Package up in a cake box or airtight container. It keeps happily for three or four days.*

The delightful simplicity of this cake, both in terms of flavor and recipe method, is where its true magic lies: it's ideal to bake with children and equally ideal to bake *for* children, as I have yet to meet one who doesn't like it. The yogurt in the batter is what gives the cake its spongy lightness. I've added chocolate chips, because vanilla crumb and chocolate pieces is such a classic, crowd-pleasing combination, but you can play around with the flavors as you please: try raisins, coarsely chopped dates and walnuts, or throw in some mixed frozen berries or a handful of fresh blueberries. Or my particular favorite: add a couple of spoons of cocoa powder to the batter, a dash of orange blossom water and some coarsely chopped Terry's Chocolate Orange for a devilishly citrussy twist.

HANDS ON TIME:
15 minutes
HANDS OFF TIME:
30–35 minutes in the oven
SERVES 8-10

4oz (100g) milk chocolate, coarsely chopped (about ½ cup)
salted butter, for the pan
2 cups (250g) all-purpose flour, plus 1 tbsp, plus more for the pan
3¼ tsp baking powder
3 eggs
¾ cup plus 1 tbsp (170g) superfine sugar
1 tsp vanilla extract
7 tbsp (100ml) vegetable oil
½ cup (120g) plain whole milk yogurt

Heat the oven to 350°F.

Tip the chocolate chunks into a bowl and chill in the freezer for 15 minutes.

Butter a 10-cup capacity bundt pan (or an equivalent-sized, deep regular cake pan) and tip it to dust all over with flour. Tip out any excess.

Combine the eggs and sugar in a large mixing bowl and whisk until doubled in volume and you have a cloud of pale yellow batter. Whisk in the vanilla extract, then add the oil and yogurt alternately, a spoonful at a time, whisking all the while, until you have a smooth batter.

Take the chocolate out of the freezer and dust with the 1 tbsp flour (this will stop the chunks sinking to the bottom when the cake bakes).

Sift the 2 cups of flour and the baking powder into a mixing bowl, then whisk in the eggy batter, a spoonful at a time. Lastly, fold in the floured chocolate.

Spoon the batter into the prepared pan and bake for 30–35 minutes, until a cake tester comes out clean when inserted to the middle of the cake. Let cool for 10 minutes or so in the pan, then turn out on to a wire rack to cool completely.

Aunt Effie's Oat Bars

🎁 *Packaged up in a cookie jar, cake box or airtight container, these keep for one week.*

These are gloriously sticky and sweet, one of my childhood favorites, but a taste that I've never grown out of (nor do I want to). The recipe is from my great aunt Effie and I relay it here in her words almost to the letter, other than to convert her ounces (so neatly written out in her elegant cursive hand) into cups and grams and to swap her superfine sugar for turbinado, because I adore the toffee-like flavor it gives. These are great to make en masse, either for bake sales or to give as gifts, because they are so delightfully simple and quick to make, yet still always a treat to eat. My one insistence is that you use quick-cooking oats rather than old-fashioned oats, which otherwise give a rather chunky consistency more like that of an overly sweet granola bar than a proper buttery, chewy oat bar.

HANDS ON TIME:
10 minutes
HANDS OFF TIME:
20 minutes in the oven;
2 hours cooling
MAKES ABOUT 16

2 sticks plus 2 tbsp (270g)
   salted butter
1½ cups (270g) turbinado
   sugar
4¼ cups (420g) quick-
   cooking oats
¼ cup (75g) Lyle's golden
   syrup
½ tsp vanilla extract

Heat the oven to 350°F. Line a 9-inch square baking pan with parchment paper.

In a medium-sized saucepan, melt the butter over a medium heat. Once the butter has melted, take the pan off the heat and add the sugar, oats, syrup and vanilla. Give everything a good stir to combine so all the oats are covered in golden, sticky syrup.

Spoon the mixture into the prepared pan and spread it out evenly, then set in the oven to bake for 20 minutes. The oat bar mixture will still be soft when you take it out of the oven.

Use a knife to cut the batch into 16 pieces, but leave to cool completely in the pan before removing.

Saffron and Raspberry Panettone 'Trifle'

🎁 *This will keep in the fridge for one or two days. On this occasion, it is probably best to drop it off in its glass trifle bowl and ask for it back after.*

This is a trifle of sorts: 'of sorts' because there is no – as you might traditionally expect from a trifle – preserves or custard involved; but still it does boast the same cheerful construction of soft cake layered with richly colored cream and fruit, and so, a trifle, if only of sorts, it is.

I make this with leftover panettone, because it's a great way to make good use of any excess over the festive period: I use about half a cake for the trifle and enjoy the other half, sliced, with coffee, or toasted for breakfast. I do love the pillowy sweet bready-ness of it. You can get all kinds of panettone these days and they all work well, but the ones that are peppered with candied peel or chocolate chips are an especially beautiful match for the jammy raspberries and rich saffron-infused mascarpone cream; if you can get your hands on a pistachio-studded cake, even better, as raspberries and pistachios are a match made in heaven. But if panettone isn't your thing, you could just as well make the trifle with pandoro – the plainer, vanilla-scented, star-shaped cousin of panettone – instead, or with slices of buttery pound cake.

Raspberries aren't in season at Christmas, of course, so it may feel incongruous to have them here, but I find you really do need the sharpness of the fruit to balance out the richness of the cream, and while they may not be local raspberries, you should be able to get hold of fresh fruit; or you could use frozen raspberries. Plus there is something about the combination of colors here – the bright red of the fruit and the intense golden yellow of the cream – that I find irresistibly festive.

This recipe contains raw eggs, so take all the usual precautions, if you need to do so (see page 70).

HANDS ON TIME:
25 minutes
SERVES 8-10

1½lbs panettone
7 tbsp water
2 tbsp Marsala
scant 1 cup superfine sugar
1 tsp saffron strands
4 egg yolks
3 cups mascarpone, at
   room temperature
⅔ cup heavy cream
3⅓ cups raspberries
   (about 14oz)

Slice the panettone into 1-inch thick pieces and set to one side.

In a small saucepan, combine the measured water with the Marsala and three-quarters of the sugar. Set over a medium heat and bring to a gentle boil. Once the sugar has dissolved and the liquid is bubbling, take the pan off the heat and set to one side.

Grind the saffron and a pinch more of the sugar together with a mortar and pestle to make a dark powder, the color of scorched earth. Spoon 2 tbsp still-warm Marsala syrup into a small bowl or cup, then add the powdered saffron and let sit for a few minutes to infuse the syrup with the flavor of the spice.

Now combine the yolks and remaining sugar in a mixing bowl and whisk until light and fluffy: you want the eggs to almost double in volume and turn a light, lemony shade of yellow. Add the mascarpone and whisk in until well combined and smooth. Lastly, add the cream and the saffron-infused syrup and whip until combined.

Cover the base of a trifle bowl with slices of panettone, then drizzle over one-third of the Marsala syrup to soak into the soft cake. Now, spoon over one-third of the mascarpone cream and sprinkle over one-third of the raspberries. Repeat with a second and third layer of panettone, syrup, mascarpone cream and raspberries. Depending on the size and shape of your bowl, you may want to create more layers (if the bowl is deep) or go for just 2 layers (if it's shallow and wide).

Chill in the fridge until you're ready to serve.

SPOIL

Some thoughts on affection, and recipes for edible presents

For me, the Christmas season officially begins when the large mixing bowls come down from the top shelf in the kitchen. I dust them off, and start making my Christmas cakes. Dried fruits steep in those bowls for days – currants, raisins, candied peel and, some years, figs and cherries too – all swimming in pungent brandy that smells so strong it permeates the house with the feeling of festivity and the promise of good things to come. Each year I bake, decorate and box up twenty-odd of these cakes to give to friends. Once one batch is done, I fill the bowls with more fruit, more brandy and start again.

It's a festive tradition I inherited from my mother: she made cakes, Christmas puddings and jars of ambrosial brandy butter to give away every year when I was growing up. I remember so clearly sitting with her in the green kitchen in the house where she still lives, perched at the tall marble table, my legs swinging under the stool as I sorted the seeds from the fat raisins (you could only buy raisins with seeds in Venice in those days) and halved the candied cherries, one by one, with a dinner knife. Somehow those tasks never felt tedious at Christmas, with carols playing in the background. This was our special thing that we did together, my mother and I.

I began baking my own cakes when I moved out: I wanted something to give for Christmas that felt spoiling and meaningful, but that I could also afford on my student budget. Some twenty years on, while my mother doesn't make her cakes any more, I still do: they've become a firm, seasonal fixture in my life. And although I bake them as gifts, the ritual of making them – if I'm honest – is really something I do for me. It's become as much a part of our holiday tradition as decorating the tree, panettone for breakfast, planning Christmas lunch or listening to the King's College choir carol service on the radio. With each stir of that intensely spiced cake batter billows forth a wave of fond, nostalgic memories.

This chapter is dedicated to food you can make to give away. You'll find no solutions here to the quandary of what to cook for dinner, unless your idea of dinner is a slice of cake and a cup of tea (and no judgement here, if that's the case, I love cake and tea). And yet, perhaps more than any other section of this book, these recipes capture its fundamental message: this is cooking for someone with the sole intention of making them feel loved.

I didn't write this chapter with any specific occasion in mind, largely because I believe you don't need a reason to give someone you love a present, just as you don't need a reason to tell them 'I love you'. Having said that, many of the recipes have a Christmas theme, because this is the time of year we tend to feel under most pressure to give something (I certainly do). And also, in some ways, it is the time of year when we are inundated with material things that we don't necessarily want or need, so to make something with your own hands and, in turn, to receive something homemade, can feel like a breath of fresh air. So, you'll find the recipes for my mother's Christmas pudding and the brandy butter to go with it (the best bit), as well as for preserves and jarred bits and bobs, which I tend to make en masse when the fruits are in season, then give away over the course of the year. But I've also included some recipes for breads, cakes and cookies – the kind of baked goods that, because of their short life span, are the sort you make with a specific and special occasion in mind – and that, unlike preserves, the making of which can be a bit of a waiting game, you can throw together when you need to improvise a present. These are gifts you can give to new parents, say, or to friends on birthdays, or quite simply to say 'thank you', 'congratulations', 'chin up' or 'I'm thinking of you'.

There's a good argument to be made that, if you don't already feel at home in the kitchen, the recipes in the pages that follow are the best place to start. With the kind of cooking and baking we cover here, timings don't really matter: there's no pressure to serve what you've cooked still warm, or to worry about how each dish might fit within the rest of your menu; no one hovers over you impatiently and hungrily. This can also be the most rewarding kind of cooking. I have friends who are impossible to buy for: usually either because they already seem to have everything or, more often, because the thing that can articulate what I want to say doesn't exist on sale in the shops. In both these scenarios, I find, giving them something they can eat and enjoy, and that I have made with love, is the happiest solution.

At the heart of the way I cook is the ardent belief that true beauty lies in simplicity. It is its very homemade-ness which will make the recipient prize your gift, so I firmly believe that it should look like you made it rather than bought it.

This adds to its magic and charm, but also takes the pressure off you. Of course, there are all sorts of fiddly, fancy things you can do with pastry bags, but a haphazardly frosted cake with fresh flowers casually strewn on top is more magical than any fondant creation with ornate piping. My great aunt Effie's shortbread – here laced with rosewater and cinnamon – is infinitely more appetizing than cookies you can buy in a box, just as a jar with a handwritten label speaks volumes more than one with a printed tag. That is not to say that you shouldn't give some thought to presentation, but I'd encourage you to find beauty in the higgledy-pigglediness of what you've made.

On a boring-but-practical note, you should always consider what your cake/cookies/preserves/what-have-you will travel in, ideally before you make them. Don't make the mistake I've made too many times, when I've lovingly baked something and then failed to get it to its intended recipient whole and in one happy and intact piece. Above all, you need some kind of container that will keep your baked goods safe and clean in transit. Obviously, it should be something you don't mind giving away: don't use your favorite plate to present the birthday cake on, beautiful as it may be, as most likely the plate won't ever find its way back to you. When I want to make an especially special gift, I'll buy something to present it on: a cake stand, for example, to serve the Certosino Christmas cake with its glimmering candied fruits, or a beautiful linen tea towel to wrap a loaf of rosemary-and-sticky-date-studded soda bread.

Mostly, though, I use disposable vessels, keeping a ready supply of these at home, so that I can improvise gifts as and when: cake boards and boxes (you can buy these in bulk online, they flat pack so are easy to store and work well for cakes, cookies, meringues and brownies); cookie jars (I mostly buy vintage from eBay and charity shops); and glass jars in all shapes and sizes. Also useful to have on hand: tissue paper (white or colored, as you prefer) which is great for lining boxes and containers, but also for bundling things up. Likewise, parchment paper and twine: you can never really have enough of these, and, if you want to jazz things up, use them to wrap the gift. And you can always think about adding a rosemary sprig, or a flower – an overblown garden rose, say – or even a Christmas tree ornament, just tied on to the parcel.

With each present, it can be a nice touch to include a little instruction note: I might scribble this on the wrapping itself, or on a brown paper luggage tag that I tie to the parcel, or on the back of a colorful postcard. On a box of brownies I might simply say 'eat within the next three days and please store in the fridge'. But with more eclectic flavors and preserves, I find it can be really helpful to offer a hint on how to serve them: so, with the Pistachio Pesto, you might include a recipe for making a good green pasta, say, or with Preserved Oranges and Lemons you might include a note with the recipe for buttery mashed potatoes, where you mash in preserved citrus to infuse the potatoes with flavor, or you might want to suggest slicing the salty, spiced preserves into thin slivers and scattering over a plate of creamy burrata cheese. It can be as simple as that.

The recipes that follow are certainly not the only dishes in this book you can give away as presents: peppered throughout these pages are countless potential gifts for all sorts of occasions. Mostly, I like to give people desserts (because I have a sweet tooth, and always assume that everyone else does too), but any of the recipes that will keep for a few days (either frozen or in the fridge) ought to be happily received. You'll find especially rich pickings on this front in the Comfort chapter.

Of course, cakes make the very best gifts of all, and while I've included only two birthday cakes in this chapter, you will find more of my favorites dotted about this book: just remember to include a little bundle of birthday candles when you drop them off.

Pistachio Butter

⊞ *Store and give away in clean, sterilized and labeled glass jars with instructions to store in the fridge for up to one month, and perhaps a little note with inspiration for how best to enjoy it (on toast, or in baking, see page 136).*

The best way I can think of describing this creamy-sweet, pastel-green confection is that it's like Nutella for grown-ups, with verdant pistachios in place of hazelnuts. It's the stuff of dreams. I love it on toast, in baking, or even by itself, devoured happily by the spoonful. Most recently, I've taken to making tiramisù (see page 123) using Pistachio Butter in place of chocolate-hazelnut spread and, on special occasions, I might even throw in a few fresh raspberries too, or, when in season, juicy, pitted cherries.

HANDS ON TIME:
10 minutes
MAKES 4 x 8-oz jars

4½ cups unsalted, roasted
    shelled pistachios
10oz white chocolate,
    coarsely chopped
    (about 2 cups)
scant ½ cup superfine
    sugar
3 tbsp vegetable oil

Sterilize 4 x 8-oz glass jars while you get on with making the Pistachio Butter. Heat the oven to 325°F. Wash the jars in hot, soapy water and set to dry in the oven for 10–15 minutes.

Combine all the ingredients in a food processor and blitz for 5–7 minutes until smooth and creamy; it should be the texture of soft butter. Pause every now and then and use a rubber spatula to scrape down the sides before blitzing again.

Spoon the Pistachio Butter into the sterilized jars; sealed, they will keep happily in the fridge for up to 1 month.

Strawberry and Vodka Preserves

🎁 *Store and give away in clean, sterilized and labeled glass jars. It will keep for up to one year.*

The addition of just a dash of vodka here is entirely frivolous: it's by no means a dominant flavor, more the subtle whisper of summer cocktails to round off the intense, heady sweetness of the strawberries.

HANDS ON TIME:
10 minutes
HANDS OFF TIME:
30–40 minutes on the stove; 15 minutes resting
MAKES 3 x 8-oz jars

2lbs 2oz strawberries, hulled, and halved or quartered, if large
3¾ cups granulated sugar
⅓ cup vodka

Sterilize 3 x 8-oz glass jars. Heat the oven to 325°F. Wash the jars in hot, soapy water and set to dry in the oven for 10–15 minutes. Combine the berries and sugar in a large pan and toss together, so all the berries are coated in sugar.

Set over a low heat to simmer gently. Once all the sugar has dissolved and the berries are swimming in clear pink syrup, a matter of 20–25 minutes, add the vodka and increase the heat to bring to a boil. Boil hard for 10–15 minutes until the mixture reaches 221°F on a candy thermometer, then turn off the heat.

If you don't have a thermometer, spoon a tiny amount on to a plate and blow on it to cool to room temperature. Once cooled, gently nudge the little pool of preserves with your finger: if ripples form on the surface then it's ready; if it still feels liquid to the touch, turn the heat back on and boil for a further 2 minutes, then test again.

Once cooked, skim the frothy, candy-floss pink scum from the surface and discard.

Leave the preserves to settle for 15 minutes, then ladle into the warm sterilized jars. Once sealed, the strawberry preserves will keep for up to 1 year.

Preserved Oranges and Lemons

✣ *Store and give away in clean, sterilized and labeled glass jars with a note on how to use them. They will keep for up to one year.*

I love preserved lemons and use them often in cooking: my most favorite trick is to scatter some thinly sliced pieces over creamy burrata cheese, but I also use them in mashed potatoes (see page 55) or sometimes, when roasting a chicken (see page 43), I'll add some very finely chopped preserved citrus to the butter I push under the bird's skin and it infuses the meat with the most delicate zesty flavor. It was while leafing through Lillie O'Brien's beautiful book *Five Seasons of Jam* that I stumbled upon her recipe for preserved mandarins, which is the inspiration for the cheerful mix of colorful oranges and lemons in a jar together here.

HANDS ON TIME:
10 minutes
HANDS OFF TIME:
3+ months maturing
MAKES 3 x 16-oz jars

1lb 2oz (4 large) lemons
1lb 2oz (about 3) oranges, preferably navel
3⅔ cups flaky sea salt, plus more if needed
6 fresh bay leaves
2 tsp pink peppercorns

Sterilize 3 x 16-oz jars. Heat the oven to 325°F. Wash the jars in hot, soapy water and set to dry in the oven for 10–15 minutes. Cut each lemon in half lengthways from top to tail, then slice lengthways to divide each lemon half into 3 long, thin slices. Do the same for the oranges.

Tightly pack the slices of mixed citrus into the sterilized jars, packing salt generously around them as you build up the layers. Poke in the bay leaves and the peppercorns, then press the fruit down well and finish with a final layer of salt.

Leave in a cool, dark place for at least 3 months before using. Turn the jars periodically: there should always be a layer of salt in the bottom, so add more if needed.

Once sealed, the jars of preserved citrus will keep for up to 1 year; once opened, keep in the fridge for a couple of months.

Pistachio Pesto

⊞ *Store and give away in a clear, sterilized and labeled glass jar with instructions to store in the fridge for up to one month, and perhaps a little note with a good recipe for pasta (see page 146).*

I like to think of this as the more savory companion to the Pistachio Butter (see page 215): the salty to its decadently sweet. Both almost outrageously creamy. The recipe method is similar and, as the two look quite same-y in a jar, do take care to label your jars carefully. You should use this as you would any pesto, tossed together with pasta, spooned over a baked potato, or spread on crusty bread and topped with juicy chopped fresh tomatoes. It also happens to be vegan. The pesto will keep happily for a month (if not longer): just keep topping it up with olive oil to cover and thus preserve the soft green paste.

HANDS ON TIME:
10 minutes
MAKES 4 x 8-oz jars

heaping 4¾ cups raw
    shelled pistachios
scant 1¼ cups skinned
    almonds
scant 1 cup olive oil, plus
    more to cover
flaky sea salt and freshly
    ground black pepper

Sterilize 4 x 8-oz jars. Heat the oven to 325°F. Wash the jars in hot, soapy water and set to dry in the oven for 10–15 minutes.

Throw both types of nuts into a food processor, then blitz until you have something that resembles wet sand. Add the olive oil and blitz again until smooth. Season to taste with ½ tsp salt and some pepper.

Spoon the pesto into the sterilized jars, making sure there is a layer of oil on top to preserve it and adding more if there is not, and store in the fridge for up to 1 month. Remove a jar from the fridge 30 minutes before using, so the pesto isn't quite as solid as it is when fridge-cold.

Mandarin and Star Anise Marmalade

🎁 *Store and give away in clean, sterilized and labeled glass jars. This will keep for up to one year.*

This tastes, looks and smells like Christmas, though I don't in any way want to suggest that the eating of it should be confined to that time of year. Marmalade on toast is always in season, and always a joyful business.

HANDS ON TIME:
25 minutes

HANDS OFF TIME:
3–5 hours, to macerate the fruit; 25–30 minutes on the stove

MAKES 3 x 8-oz jars

3¼lbs mandarins or clementines

2½ cups plus 1 tbsp granulated sugar

9 star anise

Peel the mandarins or clementines and separate into segments, removing and discarding white pith and seeds: this should give you roughly 2¾lbs fruit.

Pour the sugar into a large, ideally shallow saucepan, add the fruit and mash a little to release the juices. Now drop in the star anise and let rest for 3–5 hours to let the flavors develop.

Set the pan with the macerated fruit over a medium heat, bring to a boil, then reduce the heat and let bubble away for 10 minutes or so, until quite a lot of liquid forms and the mandarin segments are reduced in size. Take the pan off the heat, remove the star anise and use a hand-held blender to blitz the mixture until you have something that looks like thick orange juice with bits in it. You want marmalade that is slightly, pleasingly chunky in texture (if it's too smooth, it veers into the realms of orange jello).

Heat the oven to 325°F. Wash 3 x 8-oz glass jars in hot, soapy water and set to dry in the oven for 10–15 minutes.

Put the pan back over the heat, bring to a boil, then reduce the heat and let everything bubble away gently for 15–20 minutes until set. To test if the marmalade is set: spoon a tiny amount on to a cold plate, blow on it to cool, then gently nudge it with the tip of your finger. If ripples form, it's done: if it still feels liquid to the touch, give the marmalade a little longer on the stove. If you have a candy thermometer, you can also use that to test if the marmalade is ready: it should register 221°F when it's done.

Remove the pan from the heat, and, while it is still bubbling hot, spoon it into the warm sterilized jars (use a funnel if needed). Once sealed, store somewhere dark and cool for up to 1 year.

Pomegranate Jelly

⌘ *Store and give away in clean, sterilized and labeled glass jars. This will keep for up to six months.*

Seduced by the festive dark red color, a little like shimmering baubles on a tree, I most often make jars of this around Christmas, either to keep for myself and eat with turkey or goose in place of cranberry sauce, or to give to friends so that they can do the same. That said, I do find that I enjoy eating the jelly year round, most especially with lamb, but also with roast chicken or pork. It's gloriously rich in flavor as well as color, with an almost wine-like quality that cuts through fatty meat gloriously. You can easily scale the recipe up to make more, if you want.

HANDS ON TIME:
30 minutes
HANDS OFF TIME:
overnight, to macerate;
55–65 minutes on the stove
MAKES 3 x 8-oz jars

3 apples, preferably
    Granny Smith
scant 12 cups pomegranate
    seeds (9–12 fruits)
3¾ cups granulated sugar
1¼ cups water
juice of 1½ lemons

Peel, core and slice the apples into segments, roughly ½ inch thick. Combine the apple and pomegranate seeds in a large, shallow saucepan and add the sugar, then leave to macerate overnight. By morning you should have a pinkish syrup with floating pomegranate seeds in it.

Add the measured water and lemon juice. Bring to a boil, then reduce the heat to low and simmer gently for 20 minutes or so, until the apple feels soft to the touch.

Remove the pan from the heat, use a spoon to scoop off any froth that has formed on the surface, then blitz with a hand blender (or blitz the lot, in batches, in a food processor) to give a pink, smoothie-like liquid. Scoop the strawberry-hued froth from the surface and discard.

Strain through a strainer, pour back into the saucepan and set over a medium heat. Now, sterilize 3 x 8-oz glass jars. Heat the oven to 325°F. Wash the jars in hot, soapy water and set to dry in the oven for 10–15 minutes. Let the jelly bubble away for a further 35–45 minutes. Once the motion of the bubbles starts to slow down and you have something that looks like simmering honey rather than liquid, test to see if the jelly has set: spoon a little on to a cold plate and blow on it to cool. Once cooled, use the tip of your finger to nudge it gently. If ripples form on the surface, it's done; if it still feels liquid to the touch, then give the jelly a little longer over the heat. If you have a candy thermometer, you can use it to test if the jelly is ready: it should register 221°F.

Once the jelly has set, spoon it into the warm sterilized jars and seal. Stored somewhere dry and cool, it will keep for up to 6 months.

Raisins in Grappa

🎁 *Store and give away in clean, sterilized and labeled glass jars. This will keep for at least one year.*

I remember so clearly my father making this a million moons ago, when I was small and everything in the world was so very big. He kept three large glass jars on the very top shelf of the green cabinet in the kitchen, the one I couldn't reach even if I stood on a chair. The jars were filled with fat raisins swimming in clear juices, and periodically my father would lovingly check in on his jars, lifting up the heavy glass screw-on lids and topping the bloated raisins up with more grappa. His raisins tasted like fire. He liked to pour them over vanilla ice cream, to make an intensely aromatic and boozy affogato of sorts, or occasionally he would just eat them by the spoonful. Like me, my father was an impatient and greedy cook. The recipe below is slightly milder than my father's, although punchy still: I like to add a little sugar to the mix, to intensify the syrupy-ness of the juices rather than having just the grappa neat. It's not perhaps a dish for the faint of heart, but it is sheer joy for anyone who has a soft spot for rum raisin ice cream, or a boozy dessert. You can also use the raisins in baking: throw them into cake batter, something like a bundt cake (see page 198), though not perhaps if you're cooking it for or with small children, or even try them folded through a grainy, buttery polenta cake (see page 190) in place of the fresh rhubarb in that recipe.

HANDS ON TIME:
5 minutes
HANDS OFF TIME:
1–2 months maturing
MAKES 2 x 30-oz jars

8 cups raisins
½ cup granulated sugar
3¾ cups grappa

Sterilize 2 x 30-oz glass jars. Heat the oven to 325°F. Wash the jars in hot, soapy water and set to dry in the oven for 10–15 minutes. Combine the raisins and sugar in a bowl and toss together so the raisins are coated.

Divide the sugared raisins between the sterilized jars so there is only ¾ inch left between the top of the raisins and the lid of each jar. Pour half the grappa into each one, filling the jars right up to the top.

Seal and let rest for 1–2 months before opening. These keep for at least 1 year and – truth be told – pretty much forever after that.

Mimosa Truffles

❀ *To make a gift of these, package up in a small cake box or airtight container (lined with yellow tissue paper, if you like), or arrange them in a glass jar and add a label.*

March 8 is International Women's Day, and, for me, it will always be 'mimosa day'. In Italy, where I grew up, it's tradition to give the women in your life a bunch of sunny mimosa blossoms on this day: husbands to wives, mothers to daughters, sisters to sisters, friends to girlfriends, even the teachers at school will present the girls in their class with a small bunch of flowers. The reason: a celebration of the fact that you are a woman. It's a meaningful and charming tradition that I feel grateful to have grown up with. Mimosa blossoms are symbols of strength and femininity, they thrive in hostile conditions, growing into something light, cheery and sweet-scented. While the flowers might look frivolous, they are every bit as resilient and strong as they are beautiful. As far as metaphors and symbolism go, mimosa for Women's Day is a pretty inspiring one. These truffles, made with limoncello, coconut and white chocolate coated in zesty yellow crumbs, look remarkably like mimosa's pompom blossoms. They're simple to make and to give to the women you love, as a small reminder of how proud you are to have them in your life. They keep for a couple of days and are lovely after dinner with coffee or tea, or as a mid-afternoon pick-me-up.

HANDS ON TIME:
30 minutes
HANDS OFF TIME:
30 minutes in the fridge
MAKES 15–20

10oz plain pound cake
2 tbsp unsweetened
   shredded coconut
14oz white chocolate,
   coarsely chopped
   (about 2¼ cups)
2 tbsp limoncello
2 tbsp milk
8–10 drops of yellow
   food coloring

In a large mixing bowl, crumble two-thirds of the pound cake into small pieces (about 2⅓ cups). Add the coconut.

Put the white chocolate in a small heatproof bowl, then set over a pan of barely simmering water (make sure the bowl does not touch the water) and stir occasionally until melted.

Add roughly half the chocolate to the cake crumbs in the bowl, along with the limoncello and milk. Give everything a good stir with a wooden spoon, then bring the ingredients together with your hands to make a soft, doughy mixture.

Roll the mixture into little balls, each roughly the size of a small walnut, and lay them on a plate or baking sheet: you should get 15–20 balls from the mixture.

Now crumble the last of the cake into a second dish and add the food coloring. Toss the crumbs together with a fork, so that they all turn a vibrant shade of yellow.

Dip each little ball into the rest of the white chocolate so that it's entirely coated in a thin film, then roll in the yellow cake crumbs. Carefully put back on the baking sheet or a plate to set: this should take roughly 1 hour at room temperature or 30 minutes in the fridge.

Lavender and Raisin Tea Cake

⊞ *Wrap in parchment paper and tie with twine, tucking in a few lavender and/or rosemary sprigs for decoration, if you like. The cake will keep in an airtight container for up to one week.*

There are not many people in this world as kind or as gentle as was Eileen. She had a gift for making you feel safe – whatever was happening in the world – just by looking at you with her soft gray eyes. Eileen used to make what she and I called tea loaf (but everyone else, I think, calls Irish brack) for me when I was a child. Now when I bake it I always think of her, in part because the recipe I use is largely hers and recipes, flavors, tastes can be a way of holding on to that which we're sad to have lost.

A simple, yet exquisitely nice light fruit cake, here infused with a little lavender as well as tea, delicate and subtle, just a whisper of flavor lingering with each mouthful of soft, crumbling fruit. Halfway between a loaf of fruit bread (Eileen always baked hers in a loaf pan) and a rich fruit cake; it's not overly sweet (there is no added sugar in the recipe, just the sweetness from the dried fruits, which steep in tea overnight before baking). You could also try tossing in a handful of coarsely chopped dried apricots with the fruit, or omit the lavender if you don't want that floral flavor.

However you make it, tea cake makes for a wonderful gift because, like any good fruit cake, it's so rich in moisture and flavor from the fruit that it keeps happily for a good few days: you can ice it if you like with a little confectioners' sugar mixed with a dash of Earl Grey tea or lavender-infused water, or leave it plain and bake in a loaf pan as Eileen used to.

HANDS ON TIME:
15 minutes
HANDS OFF TIME:
4 hours, or up to overnight,
to steep the fruit;
60–70 minutes in the oven;
20 minutes cooling
SERVES 8–10

2 heaping tsp Earl Grey
    tea leaves
2 heaping tsp dried
    lavender
1¾ cups plus 1 tbsp (450g)
    boiling water
6 cups (750g) mixed
    dried fruits (such as
    raisins, golden raisins,
    diced candied peel)
salted butter, for the pan
1 egg
2 cups plus 2 tbsp (275g)
    all-purpose flour
3¾ tsp baking powder

Spoon the tea leaves and dried lavender into a heatproof pitcher, then add the measured boiling water and leave to cool.

Toss the mixed fruits into a mixing bowl and, when the tea has cooled, pour it over the fruit, using a fine-meshed strainer to catch the leaves. Stir a couple of times, cover with a clean tea towel and set somewhere cool to steep overnight, or for at least 4 hours.

Heat the oven to 350°F.

Butter a 9-inch springform cake pan and line it with parchment paper.

Crack the egg into a cup and beat lightly with a fork, then pour it over the fruit and mix. Now sift in the flour and baking powder and mix with a wooden spoon until well combined.

Spoon the cake mixture into the prepared pan and set in the oven for 60–70 minutes, until a knife comes out clean when inserted to the middle of the cake. Check on the cake every now and then, and, if it is browning too much on top, cover with a sheet of baking parchment.

Once baked, let cool for 10 minutes or so in the pan, then leave for another 10 minutes on a wire rack before serving, either plain as is, or with lashings of salted butter.

Rose and Cinnamon Shortbread

Package up in an airtight container or cake box lined with colorful tissue paper or parchment paper. The shortbread will keep for up to five days.

My most vivid memory of my great aunt Effie is that she was very small: even aged nine I was almost as tall as her. She wore her hair neatly coiffed and spoke with a soft, soothing Scottish accent; she was the kind of person that you always felt at home with. Part of that homey feeling was how she cooked and cared for everyone with such tangible love: I remember her afternoon teas, in the living room of her ground floor flat in Edinburgh, sitting by the roaring fire, cakes and cookies and the like laid out on trays perched on the ottoman in the middle of the room. There was malt loaf smothered in yellow butter, there were scones, homemade gingerbread loaf as well as fruit cake, and sandwiches, and always a big plate of buttery shortbread dusted in shimmering white sugar. The recipe here is Aunt Effie's: buttery, crumbly, light. She used rice flour, which you can substitute with 1 cup of cornstarch if you like, but rice flour is better. I've laced the shortbread base with a dash of rosewater and warming cinnamon, which gives it a light golden tan rather than the traditional white appearance, but feel free to omit that if you're in the mood for something plainer and comfortingly traditional. A box of these cookies makes a lovely hostess gift, or small pick-me-up to put through a friend's letterbox.

HANDS ON TIME:
10 minutes

HANDS OFF TIME:
30 minutes in the oven;
1 hour cooling

MAKES 16 wedges

2 sticks (220g) salted butter, softened, plus more for the pans

1¾ cups (220g) all-purpose flour

½ cup plus 2 tbsp (120g) superfine sugar, plus more for sprinkling

¾ cup plus 1 tbsp (120g) rice flour (or see recipe introduction)

2 tsp ground cinnamon

1½ tsp rosewater

Heat the oven to 350°F and butter 2 x 9-inch springform cake pans.

Combine the butter, all-purpose flour, sugar, rice flour and cinnamon in a food processor and blitz until you have something that resembles the consistency of wet sand. Add the rosewater and blitz again until combined.

Divide the buttery rubble between the prepared pans and press it in so you have thin, evenly distributed rounds of shortbread dough.

Bake in the oven for 30 minutes, until dry to touch and lightly golden all over; the cinnamon makes it a little tricky to see the color, but you will see it turns a more intense shade of golden brown as it bakes.

Take the pans out of the oven and, while the shortbread dough is still soft, use a knife to slice each round into 8 wedges and prick each wedge with a fork a few times. Sprinkle evenly with extra sugar. Do all this with the shortbread still in the pans and let cool and harden in the pans, too. Once cooled completely, remove from the pans.

The shortbread will keep crisp and delicious for up to 5 days in an airtight container.

Sfogliatine

Light-as-air, flaky cookies with a caramelized, feathered sugar glaze. They may seem like a little bit of a faff to make, largely because there is piping involved, but they are in no way difficult. Indeed, I can't help feel that the tops look prettier with an erratic pattern: a beautiful mess, in the same way Florentine hand-marbled papers are a pastiche of feathered, chaotic paint blobs. The recipe below is for 40 cookies, which is a lot, but they keep nicely for a week and are outrageously moreish, so I always eat more than I think I will. However, if it's too many, halve the quantity of preserves and pastry. It's tricky to halve a single egg white, so you'll find yourself with some glaze left over: you can keep this in the fridge for a couple of days and either brush it over any cookies you might be baking before they go in the oven, or, if you have more puff pastry to hand, make a few more *sfogliatine*.

HANDS ON TIME:
25 minutes

HANDS OFF TIME:
40–50 minutes in the oven
(in 2 batches)

MAKES ABOUT 40

butter, for the pans
½ cup (130g) apricot
   preserves
1½ cups (150g)
   confectioners' sugar
1 egg white
4 sheets store-bought puff
   pastry, thawed if frozen

Heat the oven to 400°F. Butter 4 baking sheets and line them with parchment paper.

Press the preserves through a strainer, then spoon it into a pastry bag and cut off the very tip, so you have the tiniest hole possible to pipe through. If you don't have a pastry bag, spoon the preserves into a corner of a plastic resealable bag and cut off the tip; it will do just as well.

In a small bowl, whisk the confectioners' sugar and egg white together to make a runny, white paste.

Now, unroll 2 sheets of the pastry and lay one on top of the other, pressing down a little as you go. Cut into 20 finger-sized rectangles. Arrange the pastry sticks on the prepared pans, leaving plenty of space between them, then use a pastry brush to generously glaze all the pastry pieces with the sugar paste.

Now pipe the preserves directly into the sugar glaze in a diagonal, to create a pattern over the cookies. I find it works best if I trail the very tip of the pastry bag in the glaze so it creates a little ridge, like a valley, to fill with preserves. Don't worry about being neat with this: the more erratic the pattern, the prettier the cookies will look.

Bake for 20–25 minutes, until all puffed up and lightly golden and caramelized on top. While the first batch bakes, repeat the process with the second 2 sheets of pastry, using the last of the preserves and the sugar paste. Let cool on the baking sheets before eating.

Chocolate and Hazelnut Cantucci

🎁 *Package up in a cookie jar or cake box, or these look beautiful in large clear glass jars; they will keep for one month.*

Cantucci are dry, crunchy cookies designed for dipping in sweet wine after dinner; I have a soft spot for dipping them in hot chocolate and coffee too. A classic Tuscan recipe, this version is made from hazelnuts, though you can try any combination of fruit and nut, from dried fig and almond to crystallized ginger and pistachio. Because they are intended to be dry – chunky, crunchy and a little chewy rather than snap-crisp – they have a remarkably long shelf life, so are ideal gifts, as you can make large batches to keep or to give away without any worry of them spoiling.

HANDS ON TIME:
15 minutes

HANDS OFF TIME:
30–40 minutes in the oven;
10 minutes cooling

MAKES ABOUT 24

1 egg, plus 1 egg yolk
¾ cup plus 2 tbsp (180g)
    superfine sugar
2 cups plus 2 tbsp (270g)
    all-purpose flour
1 tsp baking powder
2 tbsp (30g) salted butter,
    softened
½ cup (70g) hazelnuts
2oz (50g) bittersweet
    chocolate, coarsely
    chopped (about ¼ cup)
1 tbsp Marsala
1 tbsp milk (optional)
flaky sea salt

Heat the oven to 400°F. Line a baking sheet with parchment paper.

Crack the whole egg into a mixing bowl, lightly whisk with a fork, then stir in the sugar until well combined.

In a second, larger bowl, combine the flour, a generous pinch of salt and the baking powder, stir to mix. Now, using your thumbs and forefingers, rub in the butter until you have a crumb-like consistency. Toss in the nuts and chocolate, then add the egg and sugar mixture.

Stir everything together so that you have a cookie dough. It will be quite dry and crumbly, but don't panic: add the Marsala and bring it all together with your hands. If the dough still feels too crumbly, add the milk.

Divide the dough in half and roll each piece into a sausage-like shape. Put each sausage on the prepared baking sheet, leaving plenty of space between them. Lightly whisk the egg yolk with a fork, then use a pastry brush to glaze the 2 logs of dough.

Set in the oven and bake for 20–25 minutes, until lightly golden on the top. It should feel like a spongy cake when you press down gently on it. Remove the pans from the oven and let cool for 10 minutes or so.

Use a bread knife to cut the logs into slices, each roughly as thick as your middle finger.

Put the slices on their sides on the baking sheet. Reduce the oven temperature to 325°F and bake for a further 10–15 minutes, until light golden all over and dry to the touch. Cool on a wire rack.

Date and Rosemary Soda Bread

🎁 *Wrap in parchment paper, or a tea towel, tie with twine and perhaps bind in a rosemary sprig for decoration. Warn the recipient to either freeze the loaf, or eat it up within two days.*

I have Sarah to thank for this glorious loaf, which is a slightly fancier variation upon the theme of her plain soda bread, for which I gave the recipe in my last book, *A Table for Friends*. Like any soda bread, this is happily simple and intuitive to make, with no kneading or proofing or any of the things that can make the baking of bread feel like a high-maintenance sort of pursuit. It's one of those dishes that swings both ways, neither entirely savory nor sweet, but joyfully much of both, in the same family as a raisin loaf, but perhaps a little mellower and more honeyed in flavor. The rosemary is subtle but still very much there, while the chunks of date peppered through the dough are pleasingly fudgy. For the rest, I've tweaked the combination of flours from Sarah's original recipe a little. The bread really is at its very best on the day of baking (though I also enjoy it toasted and lavishly buttered in the days after) and it's quick to make, so I find I bake it most often for last-minute gifts. If, for example, I'm going to someone's house for dinner. Whatever the occasion, I can think of few things more welcome than to turn up bearing a warm loaf of bread.

HANDS ON TIME:
10 minutes
HANDS OFF TIME:
50 minutes in the oven
MAKES 1 loaf

3⅔ cups (450g) all-
   purpose flour, plus
   more to dust
½ cup (50g) quick-cooking
   oats
2 heaping tsp fine sea salt
1 tsp baking soda
1 cup (250g) buttermilk
¾ cup plus 1 tbsp (200g)
   plain whole milk yogurt
1 tbsp honey
½ cup (80g) pitted and
   coarsely chopped dates
leaves from 2 rosemary
   sprigs, finely chopped

Heat the oven to 350°F. Line a baking sheet with parchment paper.

In a large mixing bowl, combine the flour, oats, salt, baking soda, buttermilk, yogurt and honey, and stir together to combine. Add the dates and chopped rosemary and stir again.

Tip the dough out on to a clean, floured surface and shape into a large ball. Put the ball of dough on the prepared pan, dust it with flour and use a sharp knife to score deep slits, marking it into quarters.

Bake for 50 minutes until golden brown and a hard crust has formed. It should sound hollow when you tap the bottom of the loaf.

Serve warm or at room temperature, ideally with generous amounts of butter. Best enjoyed within 2 days of baking, or once the loaf has cooled you can freeze it for another time.

Certosino Christmas Cake

🎁 *This will keep for two weeks and, if given with a cake stand, makes a lovely present.*

Certosino hails from Bologna, where in the Middle Ages the monks of Certosa di Bologna baked rich spiced cakes for Christmas and where still now, around the holidays, you see shop windows fill up with cakes adorned with candied peel, like jewel-studded boxes. I love the combination of fruit, honey, pine nuts, spice, fennel seeds and an occasional pop of bittersweet chocolate. Intoxicatingly aromatic, there is nothing in the Anglo Saxon cake vocabulary that quite compares with it.

SERVES 8-10

FOR THE CAKE
butter, for the pan
1 cup (300g) honey
½ cup (100g) candied
    cherries, chopped
¾ cup (100g) diced mixed
    candied peel
¾ cup (100g) raisins
2¾ cups plus 1 tbsp (350g)
    all-purpose flour
4¾ tsp baking powder
¾ cup (100g) skinned
    almonds, chopped
⅓ cup (50g) pine nuts
½ cup (50g) unsweetened
    cocoa powder
3oz (70g) bittersweet
    chocolate, chopped (⅓cup)
1 tsp ground cinnamon
2 tsp fennel seeds
¼ tsp flaky sea salt
3 Pink Lady apples, grated
⅓ cup (80g) Marsala

FOR THE DECORATION
2 tbsp honey
5oz (140g) candied pear or
    peel, chopped (⅔ cup)
heaping ⅓ cup (80g)
    candied cherries
30 skinned almonds

Heat the oven to 350°F. Butter a 9-inch springform pan and line it with parchment paper.

Warm the honey in a small saucepan and, when it's completely liquid, take it off the heat and add the cherries, peel and raisins.

In a mixing bowl, combine the flour, baking powder, almonds, pine nuts, cocoa, chocolate, cinnamon, fennel seeds and salt. Stir together, then add the grated apple and Marsala. Stir again. Lastly, mix in the melted honey with the fruit. Mix everything together.

Spoon the cake batter into the prepared pan.

Bake in the middle of the oven for 55–60 minutes, until a knife comes out clean when inserted to the center of the cake.

Let cool in the pan for 10–15 minutes, then turn out on to a wire rack.

Once the cake is completely cooled, decorate it. Warm the honey in a small saucepan until liquid. Use a pastry brush to brush the liquid honey all over the top of the cake and decorate with chunks of candied pear or peel, cherries and almonds, so the entire surface is covered and gleaming like a jeweled box. The cake will keep in an airtight container for 1–2 weeks.

Christmas Pudding

✠ *You will need to buy British-style heatproof pudding basins or heatproof bowls to send these off in, and you will want to include cooking instructions (I write these in a Christmas card or on a luggage tag and tie it to the pudding). Then bundle each up in plain white cheesecloth, and perhaps add a sprig of holly or a single Christmas ornament to it for decoration. If stored somewhere cool and dark, these Christmas puddings keep virtually forever, and even improve with age.*

This isn't a recipe for instant gratification: it's slow cooking. No single step here is especially complicated or requires any great skill, but you do need time. Time to let the fruit steep, time to let the batter rest in its bowl overnight, time to steam the puddings for the best part of a day to develop that soft, but intensely, uniquely flavored texture. Above all, you need the time to enjoy it: time to indulge in the whole house smelling and feeling like Christmas. And because, by some eccentric law of multiplication, it's very little more time (and effort) to make many puddings rather than one, that's what I tend to do: we keep one for ourselves for Christmas Day and give the rest away.

Lastly, but most importantly, don't forget to make a wish when you're stirring the batter: that's the best bit of all.

Recipe continues overleaf

HANDS ON TIME:
35 minutes
HANDS OFF TIME:
overnight, to soak the fruit;
overnight again, to rest the
batter; 4–5 hours (for each
small pudding) or 8–9 hours
(for a large pudding) to
steam; 2–3 hours to cook on
Christmas Day
SERVES 10-12 (or **5-6** for
the smaller puddings)

4 cups (500g) mixed dried
   fruits (such as raisins,
   golden raisins, diced
   candied peel)
⅓ cup (50g) pitted and
   chopped prunes
½ cup (90g) candied
   cherries
½ cup plus 1 tbsp (110g)
   dark brown sugar
1¼ cups (290g) stout,
   plus more (optional)
   if needed
1 stick (110g) salted butter,
   plus more for the
   bowl(s)
¼ cup plus 2 tbsp (50g)
   all-purpose flour
2 cups (110g) fresh brown
   breadcrumbs
½ cup (50g) almond meal
½ tsp freshly grated
   nutmeg
1 tsp ground cinnamon
2 tsp pumpkin pie spice
2 eggs
2 tbsp dark rum, plus more
   if needed (optional)
2 tbsp brandy, to serve

Put the mixed fruits, prunes, cherries, sugar and stout into
a mixing bowl, stir well, cover with a tea towel and leave
to steep overnight. Put the butter in the freezer and leave
it there to freeze overnight also.

The next day, put the flour and breadcrumbs in a large
mixing bowl and coarsely grate in the frozen butter. Toss
the butter flakes in the flour. Add the almond meal,
spices, then the soaked fruit and any of the delectable
juices collected in the bowl.

Now, lightly beat the eggs in a cup with a fork, then
add to the mixture with the rum, if using. Stir to mix
thoroughly together. If the mixture is a little stiff, add
1–2 tbsp more stout (or rum). Now, stir for luck, cover
the bowl and leave in the fridge to rest overnight.

The next day, press the mixture into a buttered 6-cup
heatproof bowl (or 2 x 2½-cup bowls) and cover with a
double layer of parchment paper and a double layer of foil,
tied tightly with string.

Steam the large pudding in a deep saucepan half-filled
with water for 8–9 hours; this long steaming gives the
pudding its wonderful taste and texture. The smaller
puddings can be cooked for 4–5 hours. If you're cooking
multiple puddings, you can use a large Dutch oven or
a fish kettle.

Lift the pudding(s) out from the pan and let cool.
Remove and discard the parchment and foil, then cover
again in the same fashion.

On Christmas Day, steam the large pudding for a
further 3 hours (2 hours for a small pudding). Lift the
pudding out of the pan, remove the parchment and foil,
then gently turn out – upside-down so it looks like a dome
– on to a serving dish with a slight lip to catch the brandy.
Pour the brandy into a metal ladle, then hold the ladle
over the flame of a candle or a gas burner, just long enough
to heat the alcohol so it's more likely to ignite.

Use a match to set fire to the brandy and pour over the
pudding. Bring to the table flaming, then, once the flames
die down, serve with brandy butter (for homemade, see
page 249).

Brandy Butter

🎁 *Store and give away in a clean glass jar. This will keep for two or three weeks in the fridge, or it freezes beautifully.*

This is my mother's recipe for hard sauce and, while I might be biased, I can only say that it is one of pure unadulterated delight. Every Christmas she lays a bowl of this brandy-laced buttercream on the table – snowy white and piled high, more brandy butter than we could ever sensibly eat – then tops it with sugared rose petals, candied mint leaves and a shower of those tiny sugared silver dragées so reminiscent of the 1980s. It looks every bit as outrageously extravagant as the brandy butter tastes, and Christmas, as far as I'm concerned, wouldn't be complete without it. Nonetheless, even the smallest jar of homemade brandy butter is the most perfect present at Christmas time, for anyone and everyone. Traditionally, of course, you eat brandy butter with either mince pies or your Christmas pudding (see previous pages for my recipe), and, for special people, you can give the two together as a gift; but I especially love it smeared on to a slice of panettone, or on toast.

HANDS ON TIME:
5 minutes
MAKES ABOUT 2 CUPS

2 sticks plus 1 tbsp salted
    butter, softened
2½ cups confectioners'
    sugar, sifted
3 tbsp brandy

Combine the butter and sifted confectioners' sugar in a large mixing bowl and beat until smooth either by hand (with a bit of elbow grease) or with a hand-held electric mixer (for ease). Add the brandy, then beat again until combined and creamy-smooth.

Store in a glass jar for 2–3 weeks in the fridge, or 3 months in the freezer.

Panforte

🎁 *Wrap in parchment paper to keep it safe and dry, then a second decorative layer of paper (I love marbled paper) and tie with a velvet ribbon. This keeps virtually forever.*

An Italian Christmas dessert: delectably sticky and sugary, laden with dried fruits, honey, nuts and all things good, almost nougat-like in texture, then drenched in a cloud of confectioners' sugar.

HANDS ON TIME:
20 minutes

HANDS OFF TIME:
30–40 minutes in the oven;
1 hour cooling

MAKES 1

butter, for the pan
½ cup (150g) honey
1½ cups (300g) superfine
    sugar
2 cups plus 1 tbsp (260g)
    skinned almonds
¾ cup (80g) diced mixed
    candied peel
scant ½ cup (75g) pitted
    and chopped dates
scant ½ cup (75g) candied
    cherries, halved
¼ cup (50g) roughly
    chopped crystallized
    ginger
1¼ cups plus 1 tbsp (160g)
    all-purpose flour
1 tsp ground cinnamon
¼ tsp ground cloves
½ tsp pumpkin pie spice
scant ½ cup (40g)
    confectioners' sugar

Heat the oven to 325°F. Butter a 9-inch springform cake pan and line it with parchment paper.

In a medium-sized saucepan, melt the honey and sugar together over a medium heat, until the sugar is completely dissolved. Take the pan off the heat, then add the almonds, candied peel, dates, cherries and ginger.

In a second bowl, combine the flour and spices and stir, then stir the dry ingredients into the pan of sticky fruit and nuts.

Spoon the mixture into the prepared pan and spread it out evenly, using your fingers and the back of a wooden spoon. Dust with one-quarter, roughly, of the confectioners' sugar and set in the oven for 30–40 minutes, until still soft to the touch, but turning lightly golden at the edges and bubbling slightly.

Sprinkle half the remaining confectioners' sugar over the hot panforte and leave to cool in the pan. Once cool, turn out and dust the remaining confectioners' sugar over the other side. Once completely cooled, wrap in parchment paper.

Ciocolatissimo Brownies

⌘ *There is categorically no gift I would want to receive more than a box of these. They keep for up to three days in an airtight container and/or freeze beautifully.*

I have my friend Delilah to thank for this brownie recipe, which I can only describe as *ciocolatissimo* because each mouthful is like diving head-first into Willy Wonka's river of melted chocolate. Everyone has their own views on how they like their brownies: for my part, I love a crisp crust and something that more closely resembles fudge than cake in the middle, which is exactly how these come out of the oven. The dense, delectable ooey-gooeyness comes from using bread flour instead of all-purpose flour, so please don't even think of swapping it out unless you prefer a drier, spongier texture. I also have a soft spot for nuggets of milky-sweet white chocolate in my brownies, which is why I've added chunks of it to the recipe below, but feel free to replace that with bittersweet or milk chocolate shards instead (or as well); and you might want to add walnuts, chopped candied peel or a handful of dried cranberries too. Otherwise, you could just bake the brownies plain and chocolatey.

HANDS ON TIME:
15 minutes

HANDS OFF TIME:
30–35 minutes in the oven;
1½ hours cooling

MAKES 15

4oz (100g) bittersweet chocolate, finely chopped (about ⅔ cup)

1 stick plus 5 tbsp (200g) salted butter

⅔ cup (60g) unsweetened cocoa powder

4 eggs

2 cups (400g) superfine sugar

scant ½ cup (60g) bread flour

½ tsp baking powder

6oz (150g) white chocolate, coarsely chopped (about ¾ cup)

Heat the oven to 350°F. Line an 8-inch square cake pan with parchment paper.

In a small saucepan, gently melt the chocolate and butter together over a low heat. Add the cocoa and stir to combine, then leave to cool slightly. In a large mixing bowl, whisk the eggs and sugar until light, airy and lemony in color. Now gently whisk the slightly cooled melted chocolate mixture into the eggs. Fold in the flour and baking powder and lastly the white chocolate chunks.

Spoon the batter into the prepared pan. Bake for 30–35 minutes, until the top feels firm to touch and a light chocolate crust has formed.

Let cool completely in the pan (don't skip this step, tempting as it is to eat the brownies straight away, or they'll collapse as you take them out of the pan). Cut into squares before serving. The brownies will keep happily for up to 3 days, or freeze well.

Raspberry and Marzipan Cake

🎁 *Carefully package in a cake box and store somewhere cool for two or three days.*

There is no better present to give someone on their birthday than a homemade birthday cake. The recipe below is a go-to of mine, a vision of delicate, picture-perfect pink, made with raspberries rather than food coloring so you can taste the color. The marzipan sponge and frosting are both wonderfully light and fluffy and even people who think they don't like marzipan love this cake.

HANDS ON TIME:
35 minutes
HANDS OFF TIME:
50–60 minutes in the oven;
20 minutes to cool
SERVES 10–12

FOR THE CAKE
2½ sticks (300g) salted
   butter, softened, plus
   more for the pans
1¾ cups (340g) superfine
   sugar
10oz (270g) marzipan,
   grated (about 2½ cups)
8 eggs
1⅓ cups plus 1 tbsp (180g)
   all-purpose flour
2½ tsp baking powder
fine sea salt

**FOR THE FILLING
AND FROSTING**
13oz (370g) fresh
   raspberries
4½ cups (450g)
   confectioners' sugar, plus
   2 heaping tbsp
3 tbsp boiling water
4oz (120g) marzipan,
   grated (1 heaping cup)
2 sticks (230g) salted
   butter, softened

Heat the oven to 325°F. Butter and line 2 x 9-inch round cake pans.

Combine the superfine sugar, marzipan and a generous pinch of salt in a food processor and blitz to something resembling sand. Add the butter and blitz until smooth.

Add the eggs, one at a time, blitzing after each to make a smooth batter. Add the flour and baking powder and blitz again until thoroughly blended.

Divide the batter equally between the prepared pans and bake in the oven for 50–60 minutes until lightly golden on top and a knife comes out clean when inserted to the middle. Let cool in the pans for 20 minutes or so, then turn out on to a wire rack and let cool completely.

To make the frosting, combine 4oz (120g) raspberries in a food processor with the 2 heaping tbsp confectioners' sugar and blitz to a smooth purée. Strain through a strainer. Discard the seeds and set the deep pink liquid to one side. In a small bowl, add the measured boiling water to the marzipan and mix it with a fork to melt it slightly (to stop it going lumpy when added to the buttercream).

In a second, large bowl, use a hand-held electric mixer to mix the 4½ cups (450g) confectioners' sugar and the butter until pale and fluffy, then add the marzipan and beat until smooth. Add a dash of raspberry purée and beat, then add more, depending what intensity of color and flavor you like.

Spoon a large dollop of the pink frosting over the first cake and spread it out evenly, then top with a layer of fresh raspberries (reserving just a few for the top). Sandwich on top the second cake and smother with the pink frosting. Decorate with the last of the raspberries. While the cake tastes best on the day of baking, it will keep in an airtight container in a cool place for 2–3 days.

Delilah Cake

🎁 *You can of course give this to someone, though it will need very careful transportation and should be kept in the fridge and eaten within two days.*

While I often volunteer to bake a cake for friends' birthdays – indeed on occasion even do so unprompted – I hold it to be one of life's greatest honors to be asked to make a cake. This is the cake I made for Delilah's 30th birthday, at her request, and it will forever after be known as Delilah Cake. A frothy light vanilla sponge (though still moist enough to be made a day ahead without turning dry) layered with vanilla-scented meringue buttercream, slightly more elaborate to make than my usual whisk-butter-and-sugar-together-buttercream, but well worth the extra effort because it's so light and airy and spreads like velvet.

There are plenty of recipes for cake in this book – chocolate, fruit, rich, light, frosted, fancy, plain, you name it – to suit your mood, to make for your birthday, to make for dinner, or to make just because; but this one is undoubtedly a special-occasion-cake. It's for big birthdays, for weddings, for those momentous life moments, the ones you're going to remember and that call for cake: making it is a commitment, largely because of its size and scale – lots of tiers, lots of cakes piled high on top of each other in the kind of cake architecture that says 'celebration' – but it's not difficult, no single step is especially complex. You can of course reduce the quantities (or even halve them) to make something smaller and more discreet.

In terms of equipment, you'll need a candy thermometer for the buttercream: if you don't have one already, this is one of my favorite pieces of kit: it's inexpensive to buy, small to store and a godsend when it comes to making this buttercream, as well as fruit preserves.

For Delilah, I baked this with a thin layer of black cherry preserves to break up the vanilla sponge, and that is the recipe I have given you here, but you can of course use any preserves that takes your fancy. This is a special occasion cake, after all, so you must dress it up as you please. Most recently, for my own birthday, I made a version of this with hot pink roasted rhubarb in the middle; rhubarb and custardy vanilla being one of my all-time favorite combinations. Just cut a few stems of rhubarb (ideally the intensely colored younger stalks) into 1½-inch pieces and arrange in a baking pan, sprinkle generously with granulated sugar and roast in the oven, covered in foil, for fifteen minutes or so, until tender but still holding its shape. Once cooled, spoon the soft rhubarb over the layer of buttercream as you would the preserves.

HANDS ON TIME:
80 minutes
HANDS OFF TIME:
40 minutes in the oven;
30 minutes in the fridge
SERVES 20

FOR THE CAKE
1 stick plus 3 tbsp (160g)
    salted butter, softened,
    plus more for the pans
5¾ cups plus 1 tbsp (720g)
    all-purpose flour
2 tbsp plus 2 tsp baking
    powder
1 tsp fine sea salt
4 cups (800g) superfine
    sugar
1⅓ cups (290g) vegetable
    oil
8 eggs
scant 2 cups (450g) plain
    whole milk yogurt
5 tsp vanilla extract

FOR THE BUTTERCREAM
2 cups (400g) superfine
    sugar
½ cup (125ml) cold water
10 egg whites
1¼ tsp cream of tartar
7 sticks plus 3 tbsp (850g)
    salted butter, at room
    temperature, cut into
    small pieces
2½ tsp vanilla extract

FOR THE FILLING
1 cup (250g) black cherry
    preserves

Heat the oven to 350°F. Butter 3 x 10-inch springform cake pans and 2 x 8-inch springform cake pans and line them all with parchment paper.

In a medium bowl, combine the flour, baking powder and salt and set aside. In a second bowl, beat the butter and sugar until it starts to look like snow, then pour in the oil and beat until airy and glossy. Beat in the eggs, one at a time, waiting until each is fully incorporated until you add the next. Add the yogurt and vanilla and whisk until just combined. Whisk in all the dry ingredients and beat until just combined. Divide between the pans and bake for 25–30 minutes for the smaller pans and 30–35 minutes for the larger pans, until a cake tester comes out clean.

Let cool for 5 minutes in the pans, then turn out on to a wire rack and let cool completely.

Meanwhile, make the buttercream: put a scant 1½ cups (280g) sugar in a saucepan and stir in the water. Set over a medium-high heat and cook until it reaches 248°F.

In a spotlessly clean bowl, whisk the egg whites until soft peaks form, then add the last of the sugar, 1 spoon at a time, until you have a glossy, stiff meringue. Whisk in the cream of tartar. Reduce the mixer speed to its lowest so the whites are continuously moving. Once the syrup is ready, pour it into the meringue in a steady stream (don't get any on the whisk or the sides of the bowl or it will harden there). Whisk until cool: this can take 15 minutes. Then add the butter, a few pieces at a time, whisking. It will become thick and creamy. If it looks like it is curdling, whisk and it will come together. Whisk in the vanilla.

To assemble, lay a large cake on a stand. Spread a thick layer of buttercream over, then spoon over some preserves and spread out evenly. Repeat to add the second and third large cakes. Don't worry if you can see cake peeking through, you can neaten it up later.

Now, place a small cake on top, carefully centered. Top with a layer of buttercream and preserves and sandwich on the second small cake. Cover completely with buttercream, then set in the fridge to chill.

Once the buttercream feels solid to touch, cover with a last, smooth layer of velvety white buttercream. Decorate with flowers. Once assembled, it will keep for 1–2 days; keep it in the fridge if the weather is warm and wait to add the flowers until a few hours before serving.

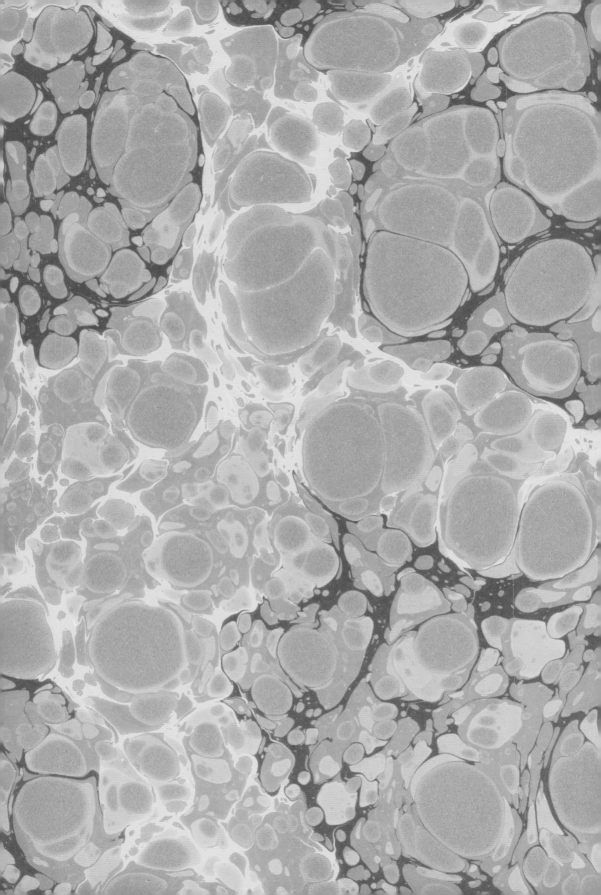

COCOON

Some thoughts on self-love, and recipes 'just' for one

The honest truth is that, as much as I enjoy the process of conjuring flour, butter and eggs into cake, the real joy for me is the moment when I cut the first slice with those who have gathered around me to eat it. For me, food is largely about the people we share it with; when I write a recipe, mostly I do so with the intention of providing something for you to enjoy with others. So my recipes will generally start with 'serves four' or 'serves six' or even 'serves eight'. Almost never 'serves one'. Except here.

It's funny how, while cooking for those we love feels completely necessary, cooking for ourselves can often feel like an expendable luxury. One of the prevailing emotions that defines food in our lives is love, but its counterpart is guilt. Just as love feels strongest when I'm eating with others, guilt feels most overpowering when it's just me eating alone, as though the time – that excruciatingly precious commodity – would be better spent tackling my to-do list; as though I don't really deserve to pause for dinner, let alone cook it for myself.

If I were to try to capture a mood for this chapter, it would be an inward-looking one, something more along the lines of what the Ancient Greeks called *Philautia*, or what we might translate as 'self-love'. I've called it 'cocoon', because that's what I most often crave, most especially when I'm alone: food that makes me feel safe, rested, cared for and simultaneously capable. Such a rainbow of emotions in something so simple as a plate of indulgently creamy pasta, or kale swimming in spices and tomato then topped with a soft runny-yolked egg.

Recently I've found comfort, optimism, relief even, in the mundane act of making an occasion out of my meals, doing it properly, even when there's no one around to share it with. I wouldn't be honest if I didn't admit that I am new to cooking this way, but what has surprised me is how much I have come to enjoy it. My hope is that this chapter will help reframe how you think about the business of cooking for yourself, too, and prompt you to answer the insidious little voice that whispers 'why bother, it's just me?' with a kind but firm, 'well, it's because it's me that it is most especially worth the bother'.

Which is why you'll find many recipes for dessert in this chapter too. This feels a little controversial. I perpetually find myself conflicted by the desire to be healthier and eat healthier, but also quite frequently end up overcome by cravings and dive deep into the cookie jar. The fast dessert recipes in these pages taste better than what lingers in my cookie jar, and as each is laid out properly on a plate, or in a bowl, they also help with sensible portion control. And so, on balance, a proper dessert to follow my solo meal is probably healthier than not. More importantly, I would never skip dessert when friends come for dinner, and, frankly, it seems a shame not to live by the same philosophy when it's just me. In fact, especially when it's just me.

Cooking for one can feel at once like the easiest and the hardest thing to do. On the one hand, you're not catering to a multiplicity of tastes, rather you're looking only to satisfy the whims of the one person in the world you know better than anyone else. It's not logistically arduous in the way that cooking for a crowd can be, and there's little washing up. On the other hand, we face a different kind of challenge, an emotional one: it can feel lonely to eat alone. I love to go out to a restaurant and indulge in an extravagant three-course meal, but I love doing so with friends, not by myself. At home, when I'm with the boys, we eat round the long and ever-so-slightly wobbly wooden table in our kitchen, but when it's just me, I carry my food on a tray and eat it curled up on the living room sofa. Somehow it seems to taste better that way. I don't know if this set-up is a way of glossing over the absence of my much-loved eating companions, or a celebration of happy solitude; perhaps a little of both.

I have friends who plan out their weekly menus down to a tee; they say that doing so makes it easier to cook over the course of the week, because it spares them from worrying about shopping and so forth once the week is in its full, busy flow. That works well for them – and it might well work well for you – but I like to start thinking about dinner when I've finished lunch. I simply don't know on Sunday night what I'll feel like eating for lunch on Tuesday or dinner on Thursday.

When I'm cooking for lots of people I do have to plan things, as it's too complicated otherwise, but when it's just me, I relish the luxury of not doing so. I keep my kitchen well stocked and have plenty on hand to improvise with: good-quality canned fish, eggs, bread that even if stale I can turn into toast, hard cheese, pasta, lemons, frozen vegetables (peas, fava beans, spinach), a bag or two of kale or salad leaves and, ideally, herbs.

Maybe a package of puff pastry sheets. Plus a few bars of chocolate and some ice cream. This way I find I have what I need to make a happily satisfying meal for myself and I'm able to comfortably tread that welcome path between premeditation and spontaneity.

A discussion of food for one wouldn't be complete without some mention of leftovers: I have a very soft spot for leftovers, and one of the things I enjoy most about eating by myself is that I can indulge fully and wholeheartedly in eating them, because while whatever it is might not quite stretch to a meal for four or five second time round, there's usually a generous enough portion just for one. Writing a recipe to make use of leftovers is of course tricky, because by definition no two lots are ever the same so it's difficult to be in any way prescriptive or precise. Even so, you'll find a few of my favorites here: a *saltata di risotto*, where you re-fry buttery risotto into a crisp pancake, or my go-to kale, cranberry and chicken salad, which makes great use of any leftovers from a roast. Cooking for yourself doesn't have to be arduous and sometimes can just be a matter of jazzing up or stretching out what you already have in the fridge.

This is a book about love, people and food. There is no intended hierarchy among the chapters, just as no single recipe is inherently better or more valuable than another. At different points in our lives we may find ourselves leaning more heavily on the contents of one chapter than another: right now, for example, I have a three-year-old and a ten-year-old to take care of; nourishing my family is what I spend the lion's share of my time and energy doing. Yet I imagine that, as the boys grow older (and so do I), what and how I cook for them will change, just as what and how I cook (and who I cook for) has in many ways changed already over the course of my life.

Yet of all the chapters, this last one should be a constant: it is important always to remember to care for yourself, however busy you are, however many other people crave your attention, however much you care for them and want to take care of them. Above all these are recipes for you: some are bursting with nutrients, some (most, really) are quick and easy to make, some quite simply are very spoiling to eat, but my hope is that they will all make you feel good, most especially on those days when you really need it.

Spinach and Lemon Soup

🎁 *Store in disposable paper soup cups (I buy mine in bulk online) or an airtight container in the fridge for two or three days and reheat as needed. Otherwise, you can freeze it.*

I first stumbled across this recipe (or an iteration of it) in my dog-eared copy of Claire Macdonald's wonderful *Seasonal Cooking*. I instantly found myself craving it, as I love both spinach and lemon but had never thought to combine the two, least of all in a soup. While perhaps not the most delicious-looking concoction, as the spinach turns a slightly sludgy shade of green when it cooks, I promise that the taste is exquisite: creamy, but pleasingly fresh, like balm for the body as well as the soul. Claire's recipe calls for the addition of a spoonful of ground turmeric, which is both warming and health-giving should you want to add some, but there is something about the unmuddled simplicity and purity of flavor of the lemon and intense green spinach that I just love, so I tend to leave it out. I don't thaw the spinach before cooking because I rarely have the forethought to do so; instead I just warm it in the pan until thawed, which elongates the cooking time by a little, but not much. If you are more organized than me and have thought ahead, you can skip that step, just add the spinach, thawed, with the lemon zest and juice, cover with broth and let simmer away for five or ten minutes or so. And while this recipe is to serve just one, you can easily increase the quantities: I love having leftovers to make for a meal another day, which I tend to freeze in a plastic container (in individual portions so I always have just enough).

HANDS ON TIME:
20 minutes
SERVES 1 generously

1 tbsp olive oil
½ onion, chopped
9oz frozen spinach
2 wide strips of lemon zest, pared with a vegetable peeler, plus finely grated zest, to serve
juice of ¼ lemon
scant 1½ cups vegetable broth
dollop of crème fraîche or heavy cream (optional)
flaky sea salt and freshly ground black pepper

Heat the oil in a saucepan, then add the onion and a generous pinch of salt. Cook gently for 3–5 minutes, until softened and translucent.

Add the frozen spinach and cook for 10 minutes until it has thawed completely. Now add the pared lemon zest and juice and cover with the broth.

Bring to a boil and simmer very gently for 5 minutes, then take off the heat, season to taste and blitz until smooth with a hand blender (or let cool and blitz in a food processor).

Serve warm with a sprinkling of lemon zest and a dollop of crème fraîche or heavy cream, if you like.

Apricot, Walnut and Halloumi Salad

Another of my friend Sarah's brilliant recipes. This is a quick-fix warm salad that always hits the spot. In the summer months, I make it with apricots, wonderfully sweet and juicy in contrast with the salty cheese, but you could just as well make it with slices of peach, yellow nectarine or red wine-hued plum. Alternatively, if stone fruit is out of season, apple is lovely too.

HANDS ON TIME:
10 minutes
SERVES 1

4oz halloumi cheese
2 apricots
2 handfuls of arugula
leaves from a small bunch
    of mint
2 tbsp olive oil
handful of walnut halves
flaky sea salt

Slice the halloumi into ¾-inch thick pieces. Halve the apricots, remove and discard the pits, then slice the halves into wedges.

Toss the arugula and mint leaves together in a dish.

Heat 1 tbsp oil in a large frying pan over a medium heat, then add the slices of cheese and apricot to the pan. Fry for 1–2 minutes on each side, until the cheese is lightly golden and the apricot is burnished.

Toss the fruit and cheese in with the salad leaves and drizzle over the last of the olive oil. Crumble over the walnuts, season to taste with a little salt and eat straight away while the cheese is still warm and soft.

Arugula, Almond and Date Salad

Every time I eat this salad, it takes me back to that shady spot in Marrakech, in the cloistered courtyard of a riad, sitting under a towering palm tree, where I first tried this, or a salad that is very similar, at least, to the recipe below. Fresh, peppery arugula leaves tossed with heaps of minerally parsley, nuts and juicy fat dates dressed in something honeyed and lightly spiced. So obsessed was I with this salad that, as soon as I returned home, I spent days playing around in the kitchen trying to recreate it. I'm delighted to say that I think I eventually got there. I will happily sit and indulge in a big bowl of this all to myself, just as is - the green leaves peppered with the fruit and nuts - but if you want to stretch the meal out a little further, you could add some leftover cold chicken, just shredded and tossed with the leaves, or, my favorite, smoked mackerel fillet, in pieces and tumbled in with the leaves.

HANDS ON TIME:
5-10 minutes
SERVES 1

2 tbsp olive oil
1 tbsp white wine vinegar
1 tsp honey
½ tsp paprika
½ tsp ground cumin
2 handfuls of arugula
leaves from a small bunch
    of parsley
small handful of raw
    almonds, coarsely
    chopped
4 medjool dates, pitted and
    coarsely chopped
flaky sea salt

In a small cup, combine the oil with the vinegar, honey and spices. Whisk it all together with a fork to make a thick, syrupy dressing.

Toss the arugula and parsley together with the nuts and dates in a bowl.

Drizzle the dressing over the salad and toss again. Season to taste with a little salt.

Radicchio, Pear and Walnut Salad

There is something so gratifying about a big bowl of these bitter, deep-red leaves, most especially when paired with juicy, sweet chunks of pear and buttery walnuts. It's the most welcome burst of color in the dreary winter months, when radicchio is at its peak and color is hard to come by. It's also what I eat when I'm craving robust, punchy flavors, something with an intense taste to savor in my mouth. The dressing is light and delicate, basically just olive oil, as the leaves themselves need so little doing to them.

HANDS ON TIME:

5 minutes

SERVES 1

½ head of radicchio di
   Chioggia or Verona
   (roughly 9oz)
½ pear
handful of walnut pieces
⅓ cup crumbled
   Gorgonzola cheese
2 tbsp olive oil
flaky sea salt

Chop the radicchio into strips and the pear into chunks. Combine in a dish. Now add the walnuts and scatter over the Gorgonzola.

Drizzle over the olive oil, season generously with salt and toss together.

Baked Eggs with Spinach and Gorgonzola

There is something so wonderfully satisfying about this recipe and its perfect one-dish completeness: the still-just-runny egg yolks swimming in creamy, pungent cheesy sauce, and the pocket of rich green wilted spinach hidden like treasure at the very bottom of the dish. It's one of those recipes for which you can easily scale the quantities up or down by adding more eggs and cheese (and spinach, of course), depending on how many people you're cooking for and how hungry they all feel. I usually go for two eggs just for me and often I enjoy it with a slice of buttered toast or a chunk of baguette on the side. Though these are by no means necessary – just happy indulgence – as the eggs are plenty filling enough.

HANDS ON TIME:
20 minutes
HANDS OFF TIME:
10–14 minutes in the oven
SERVES 1

1 tbsp olive oil
7oz frozen spinach
1 heaping tbsp salted
   butter
⅔ cup crumbled
   Gorgonzola cheese
2 eggs
⅓ cup heavy cream
flaky sea salt and freshly
   ground black pepper

Heat the oven to 400°F.

Heat the oil in a small ovenproof saucepan over a medium heat, add the frozen spinach and cook until thawed, 10–12 minutes, stirring every so often. Take the pan off the heat, add the butter and half the Gorgonzola and stir through until melted (a few whole chunks of cheese are fine, but you want the cheese mingled in with the green leaves). Season to taste with salt and pepper.

Use the back of a spoon to make 2 small hollows in the bed of cheesy spinach, then crack an egg into each hollow. Dot the last of the Gorgonzola over the spinach and pour in the cream.

Top with a few grinds of pepper and set in the oven for 10–14 minutes, until lightly golden on top and the egg whites are opaque.

Lemony Chickpea and Walnut Salad

Store in an airtight container or glass jar for two or three days in the fridge. As well as a welcome doorstep gift, this makes a lovely dish for picnics or box lunches.

Milli cooks chickpeas this way, just with a little onion, then heaps and heaps of lemon (both the zest and juice) and it was at her idyllic Sussex cottage, sitting in the nook in the kitchen by the window, that I first tried chickpeas done Milli's way. I can't tell you how unbelievably good they are. Milli uses dried pulses: she soaks them in cold water overnight, then brings the chickpeas to a boil – with just a dash of baking soda in the pan to stop them breaking up – and cooks them on the stove for roughly two hours. I must admit that I use chickpeas from a jar, which are perhaps a little less tasty, but only marginally so, and on balance I'm happy to make a quasi-imperceptible compromise on flavor in exchange for the instant gratification I get out of throwing dinner together in a matter of minutes. The secret is to buy the kind that come in a jar rather than a can and to make sure to wash them thoroughly under running cold water to do away with any of the gunk which makes them turn gloopy as you cook them. To the buttery-beige chickpeas, I add extra lemon, a shower of verdant parsley and a handful of crunchy walnuts. And if I'm craving something more substantial, I'll add a can of meaty tuna (drained, of course), or a boiled egg – the yolk still sunshine-yellow and jammy in the middle – to the dish.

HANDS ON TIME:
15 minutes
SERVES 1

1 cup drained chickpeas, from a jar
1½ tbsp olive oil
1 small onion, chopped
finely grated zest and juice of ⅓ lemon
leaves from a small bunch of parsley, chopped
handful of walnuts
flaky sea salt and freshly ground black pepper

Put the chickpeas in a colander and run them under cold water to wash them clean. Keep running water over them until the water is clear and no longer frothy.

Heat the olive oil in a saucepan over a medium heat. Add the chopped onion and a generous pinch of salt. Fry gently for 3–5 minutes until the onion softens and turns translucent.

Add the chickpeas and toss together in the pan, just long enough to heat through.

Now, remove from the heat and add the lemon zest and juice. Toss together. Lastly, sprinkle over the parsley and crumble in the walnuts.

Toss together for a final time, season to taste and serve warm or at room temperature, as you like.

Black Rice, Roasted Garlic and Green Olive Salad

🎁 *Store in an airtight container or glass jar for two or three days in the fridge. Again, this is a great recipe to take along for picnics or packed lunches.*

In Italy, we call this kind of black rice *riso Venere* or 'Venus rice', named after the Roman goddess of love, because once upon a time it was thought to be an aphrodisiac. It's a wholegrain black rice that tastes slightly chewy and deliciously, moreishly nutty. Intensely colored, it has a way of turning the cooking water a violent shade of burgundy that I find oddly pleasing; but be wary, as it does stain. I love the flavor: I'll often cook more rice than I need, then keep it in a bowl in the fridge. As the days go by, either I eat the rice just dressed with a little olive oil as a side dish to fish, chicken or what have you, or I'll toss the grains with whatever I have to hand – boiled eggs, cherry tomatoes, slivers of fennel, a can of tuna, avocado, chopped raw zucchini, a handful of pomegranate seeds, lima beans and so on – to make various salads of sorts. This particular combination with buttery-sweet roasted garlic, briny green olives and a fair amount of parsley leaves is my particular favorite. I'm normally not a huge fan of garlic and I use it little in my cooking, but here the cloves are roasted to the point that they taste almost caramelized and melt-in-your-mouth tender. It's bliss.

HANDS ON TIME:
15 minutes

HANDS OFF TIME:
45 minutes while the rice bubbles away on the stove and the garlic roasts

SERVES 1

1 head of garlic
2–3 tbsp olive oil
generous ⅓ cup black
   Venus rice
small handful of pitted
   green olives, halved
leaves from a small bunch
   of parsley, chopped
flaky sea salt and freshly
   ground black pepper

Heat the oven to 350°F. First roast your garlic: slice the top off the head of garlic and sit it on a sheet of foil, drizzle over 1 tbsp olive oil, season generously with salt and pepper, then wrap the garlic up in the foil and set in the oven to roast for 45 minutes, until tender.

Meanwhile, cook the rice: using a medium saucepan, tip in the rice and a generous pinch of salt and cover with roughly 6 cups cold water: the ratio of rice to water matters little, but there should be plenty of water in the pan, as if you were cooking pasta. Set over a high heat and bring to a boil, then reduce the heat and let it bubble away gently for 30–35 minutes, until the rice is tender and chewy. Strain the rice in a colander, dress with 1–2 tbsp olive oil and set aside.

Let the garlic cool a little, then peel the skins off each clove and add to the rice.

Add the olives and parsley, then toss together. Season to taste with a little more salt and pepper, if you like, and eat at room temperature.

Fried Mozzarella Balls

This is the kind of recipe that's just too much of a faff for me to enjoy cooking on a large scale, but scaled back for one, it's simply perfect. In fact an excuse to eat this kind of food is why I love to eat by myself. Yes, it does involve some degree of effort, though by no means a herculean one, and I find the ritual of dipping the mozzarella in egg, then rolling it in breadcrumbs, to be a pleasingly mechanical business, the kind of thing I'll happily do while listening to the radio or an audiobook, or while chatting to a friend on the phone (on speaker, of course), all of which, for the right day and the right mood, is kind of a treat in itself. Moreover, because there are only so many of the mozzarella balls that a single person can actually eat – delicious though they are – it also doesn't take very long to do. If you like, you can also freeze the mozzarella balls once they're prepared, so you have a stash ready to go for a quick-fix meal whenever you fancy it.

Don't be intimidated by the deep frying: the instructions here are foolproof and a deep saucepan will protect you from any spitting oil, should there be any. For me, the fried mozzarella – oozing-melted in the middle and encased in a shell of golden breadcrumbs – is a meal in itself and needs little else with it: I might add some crisp, bitter salad leaves on the side and then I'm good to go. If I can get my hands on the miniature mozzarella pearls, or *ciliegine*, tiny and perfectly spherical, I use those, if only because they look so perfect on the plate; otherwise just a normal fresh mozzarella ball cut into small chunks works every bit as well.

HANDS ON TIME:
15 minutes
SERVES 1

6oz fresh mozzarella,
   mozzarella pearls
   or *ciliegine*
1 egg
1 tbsp milk
2 tbsp all-purpose flour
¼ cup panko breadcrumbs
vegetable oil, for deep
   frying
flaky sea salt and freshly
   ground black pepper

If using a large mozzarella ball, cut it into smaller pieces. Put the pieces – or the small mozzarella pearls or *ciliegine*, if you have those – to drain in a strainer for a few minutes.

In a small shallow dish, combine the egg and milk, season generously with salt and pepper and beat lightly with a fork. In a second shallow dish, pour out the flour, and in a third dish, the breadcrumbs.

Dip each piece of mozzarella in the flour, then roll it in the egg mixture and lastly in the breadcrumbs. I like to stick them with a fork so that it's easy and not too messy to dip them in and out.

Heat about 2 inches of oil in a deep fryer or deep saucepan over a medium heat and bring it to 325–350°F. If you don't have a thermometer, you can test the temperature by dropping a small cube of bread into the pan: it should sizzle and turn golden within 30 seconds. If it browns more quickly, reduce the heat a little, or if it takes longer, just wait a little while before frying the mozzarella.

Once the oil is hot enough, carefully lower the mozzarella pieces or balls into the hot oil and fry until golden brown all over. This should take 1–2 minutes.

Drain the fried mozzarella on paper towels, then sprinkle with a little salt and eat while piping hot.

Ravinder's Kale with Egg

This recipe, one of my favorites in this chapter, comes by way of my dear friend and brilliant chef, Ravinder Bhogal. Ravinder has a way of cooking her greens – in a light tomato sauce and peppered with turmeric, cumin and coriander seeds, then laced with just a dash of sharp lemon juice – that is unbelievably good, good in a way that I never thought vegetables could quite taste. The recipe below is loosely adapted from Ravinder's for *sukuma wiki*, or collard greens: I use kale in place of the collard greens, because I find it easier to come by and often have a bag kicking around in the fridge. I've also added a soft-boiled egg, the yolk still jammy in the middle, on top, because the two together – the wilted, tomatoey veggies and the egg – are for me the most perfectly complete dinner. Most especially when enjoyed in a deep bowl, sitting curled up on my sofa, ideally watching the kind of trashy TV that I would never dream of owning up to viewing in polite company.

HANDS ON TIME:
15 minutes
HANDS OFF TIME:
10 minutes on the stove
SERVES 1

1 egg
1 tbsp olive oil
½ onion, chopped
½ tsp coriander seeds
¼ tsp ground cumin
⅓ cup cherry or grape
   tomatoes, halved
3oz (about 3 large stalks)
   curly kale, coarse ribs
   removed
juice of ¼ lemon
flaky sea salt and freshly
   ground black pepper

Put the egg in a small saucepan and cover with cold water. Bring to a rolling boil over a high heat. The moment the water starts to gallop, cover the saucepan and take it off the heat. Leave the egg in the water for 8 minutes exactly, then drain the water and gently peel the egg.

While the egg is cooking, heat the oil in a frying pan and gently fry the onion for 4 minutes or so, until it turns golden. Now, add the spices and fry for 1–2 minutes until they become aromatic. Add the tomatoes and cook for a further 3–5 minutes, until they begin to break down. Lastly add the greens, cover the pan and braise them for 10 minutes.

Once cooked, season the leaves to taste and add the lemon juice. Spoon into a bowl or dish and top with the egg.

Kale, Chicken and Cranberry Salad

I often make a big bowl of this salad, or a slightly simpler version of it, to go with lunch or dinner for the family: just the frilly kale leaves, drenched and tenderized in their mellow creamy dressing, then tossed with slivers of crisp, sweet Pink Lady apple and a handful of walnuts crumbled in for extra crunch. I love it. But when I'm by myself, and if salad is all I have for dinner, then I want something a little more meaty, more substantial to eat, which is how this variation – with the addition of juicy shredded roast chicken and peppered with ruby-red dried cranberries – came to be a firm favorite and a staple of my solo supper repertoire. It's a great way to use up any leftover roast chicken, or, at Christmas time, I have been known to make it with leftover turkey too. You could of course use walnuts instead of pecans, but I do love the subtly candied flavor of pecans and their glossy appearance, especially with the slightly sour cranberries.

HANDS ON TIME:
5-10 minutes
SERVES 1

2oz (about 2 large stalks)
   curly kale, coarse ribs
   removed
½ tsp tahini
½ tsp red wine vinegar
1 tbsp olive oil
⅓ cup shredded cooked
   chicken
small handful of pecans
small handful of dried
   cranberries
flaky sea salt

Toss the kale leaves into a bowl. Drizzle over the tahini, vinegar and olive oil and massage the leaves with your hands for a few minutes, until they're all covered in the dressing; you should feel the leaves wilt and soften as you massage them. Season to taste with a little salt.

Toss the chicken in with the green leaves.

Crumble over the nuts, tip in the cranberries and toss again before eating.

Penne with Saffron Cream

Pasta is the dream to cook for one: it's quick, it's easy and most recipes can easily be scaled up or down as needed. Any of the pasta recipes in this book I would happily cook just for me and adjust the quantities accordingly, but penne served this way – swimming in an indulgently creamy, sunshine-yellow sauce – is my favorite, which is how this recipe in particular ended up in this chapter. Even for a pasta, it is ridiculously easy to make; I love the glorious one-pan-ness of it and I love the intensity of the saffron. There is no reason why the pasta shapes should be penne, other than personal preference; I find that the little tubes have an excellent way of filling up with the creamy sauce that is especially pleasing.

It may seem like an extra faff to grind the saffron strands into powder here, but it's really not, it takes moments to do and makes a tangible difference to the intensity (both of color and flavor) of the sauce. If you prefer, you can also buy saffron powdered – it's just a little trickier to find, though many online vendors will have it and you may find it worth bulk buying – and skip the step.

HANDS ON TIME:

5 minutes

COOKING TIME:

10 minutes on the stove

SERVES 1

⅔ cup penne

½ tsp saffron strands

2 tbsp heavy cream

1 heaping tbsp grated
   Parmesan cheese

1 heaping tbsp mascarpone

flaky sea salt and freshly
   ground black pepper

Bring a medium-sized saucepan of generously salted water to a boil. When the water begins to gallop, cook the pasta *al dente*, follwing the package instructions.

Meanwhile, combine the saffron strands with a pinch of salt in a mortar and pestle and grind into a fine, intensely red powder.

Scoop half a cup of the cooking water out of the pasta pan and set to one side.

When the pasta is done, drain in a colander and toss back into the pan. Now add the saffron, cream, Parmesan and mascarpone, along with a little of the reserved cooking water (2 tbsp or so should do), and stir together so all the pasta is coated in the yellow sauce and the cheese is completely melted.

Season with pepper and eat while still piping hot.

Spaghetti with Pistachio and Lemon

This is one of those dishes I could happily cook for a larger party, but I enjoy eating it so much I always want to cook it for myself; the fact that it's so simple and quick to throw together means that I happily do so often. I especially love how the lemon zest tenderizes and caramelizes ever-so-slightly in the pan and just infuses the pasta with flavor: it tastes like a balmy summer's evening.

HANDS ON TIME:
10 minutes
SERVES 1

3oz spaghetti
1 lemon
2 tbsp olive oil
¼ cup raw shelled
    pistachios, plus more
    to serve
flaky sea salt

Bring a large saucepan of generously salted water to a boil. When the water begins to gallop, add the spaghetti and cook *al dente*, following the package instructions.

Use a vegetable peeler to cut 2–3 wide strips of zest off the lemon, slice them into fine strips, then the strips into pieces about ¾ inch long. Do a few extra as well, if you'd like to sprinkle some unfried zest over the top of the pasta.

Heat the olive oil in a medium frying pan over a medium heat, add the slivers of lemon zest with a generous pinch of salt (reserving any zest you want to serve on top) and fry gently for 4–5 minutes, until softened and the kitchen starts to smell of lemon.

Reserving a few for decoration, chop the pistachios finely and add them to the pan with the lemon. Fry gently for 1–2 minutes. Squeeze the juice of ½ lemon over the nuts, then spoon a scant ladleful of the pasta cooking water into the pan. Let the nuts simmer away for a few minutes until the liquid has largely evaporated.

Drain the pasta in a colander, then toss into the pan with the lemon and pistachio. Take the pan off the heat and toss the spaghetti well so that it is all coated in sauce. Sprinkle with a few chopped pistachios and a sliver or so of unfried lemon zest, if you like, before serving.

Salmon en Papillote

This is just such a pretty way of cooking fish: I still get a thrill – a disproportionately large one – from opening up the little paper parcel to eat my salmon fillet, steamed and cooked to tender pink perfection. If in season, I'll throw a few asparagus spears in there to steam with the fish, which makes for a complete meal; otherwise, or sometimes in addition, a little salad on the side (tomato or green leaf). And if I have any leftover mustardy potatoes kicking around in the fridge (see page 56), I'll eat those at room temperature with my fish, hot and straight from the oven.

HANDS ON TIME:
5 minutes
HANDS OFF TIME:
15 minutes in the oven
SERVES 1

handful of baby asparagus
   spears (optional)
1 salmon fillet
3 lemon slices
1 tbsp olive oil
leaves from a few sprigs
   of parsley
flaky sea salt and freshly
   ground black pepper

Heat the oven to 350°F.

Arrange the asparagus on a large sheet of parchment paper. Put the salmon fillet on top of the asparagus, then lay the lemon slices, overlapping, on top of the fish. Drizzle with the olive oil and season with salt and pepper. Top with the parsley.

Fold the paper like a parcel, sealing the corners underneath, then place on a small baking sheet.

Set in the oven for 15 minutes, just until the salmon turns opaque. Eat with the lemon slices, parsley and just-cooked asparagus.

Saltata di Risotto

I learned about the joys of *saltata di risotto* – a golden, crisp pancake of refried, leftover risotto – from my mother, who in turn learned it from a friend in Rome. In Italian it literally translates as 'jumped', 'skipped' or 'flipped' and that's what you do: fry it and flip it in the pan so it turns crisp on both sides. As a child, the biggest treats were those days when *saltata* was happening in the kitchen: the smell of it, the intense sound of it sizzling in the pan, the anticipation before the pancake flip. Still now, some thirty-plus years on, it tastes like happiness on a plate, so much so that I always try to make extra risotto so that we (or I) have enough for this the next day. Like all recipes for making use of leftovers, the quantities below are intended as a guide rather than being in any way prescriptive; really what you have is a set of principles for cooking the *saltata* and the rest is up to you. My only caveat is that if you go too large with the pan and the pancake, it tends to collapse when you flip it: it still tastes glorious, but doesn't look quite so good.

HANDS ON TIME:
15 minutes
SERVES 1

1 tbsp olive oil
3 tbsp grated Parmesan
    cheese
heaping ¾ cup leftover
    risotto (see page 34
    for a recipe)

Heat the oil in a medium-sized frying pan over a gentle heat. Sprinkle half the Parmesan over the center of the pan: you want a round covered with Parmesan. Spoon the leftover risotto over the Parmesan and use the back of your spoon to press it down into something that resembles a compact, thick pancake (typically, mine looks something like a 5-inch-wide disc, roughly ¾ inch thick).

Let it fry gently for 5–7 minutes, until the rice is hot all the way through and the underside is golden brown.

Use a spatula to gently prize the risotto pancake off the pan, then flip it on to a plate: I do this by taking the pan off the heat momentarily, laying a plate over the risotto pancake, using one hand to hold the plate in place and the other to flip the pan.

Now sprinkle the last of the Parmesan over the middle of the pan again and gently slip the *saltata*, cooked-side up, back into the pan.

Fry gently for a further 4–5 minutes until the underside is crisp and golden also. Then gently slip it out of the pan and on to a plate, and eat while still burn-your-mouth hot.

Roast Cornish Hen with Lemon Potatoes

This is essentially roast chicken for one, perfectly portioned and with potatoes in the pan too. Because some days you need the comfort of a roast chicken and because eating alone is no reason to be deprived of that happy solace. To complete the meal, you might perhaps want a few dressed salad leaves, and, of course, a nice dessert; any of those in the pages that follow will do perfectly.

HANDS ON TIME:
15 minutes
HANDS OFF TIME:
45–60 minutes in the oven
SERVES 1

2 medium-sized potatoes
  (about 9oz)
½ lemon, sliced into
  4 wedges
a few rosemary sprigs
1 Cornish hen
1 tbsp salted butter,
  softened
¼ cup olive oil
flaky sea salt

Heat the oven to 400°F.

Chop the potatoes into roughly 1-inch chunks, toss them into a saucepan, cover with cold water and add a generous pinch of salt. Bring to a boil over a medium heat, then cook for 5 minutes and drain in a colander.

Meanwhile, stuff 1 lemon wedge and a couple of rosemary sprigs into the Cornish hen, smother the skin with the butter and season generously with salt. Put the bird in a small roasting pan and nestle the potatoes around it, along with the last of the rosemary and lemon wedges and the oil, tossing the potatoes in the oil and flavorings.

Roast in the oven for 45–60 minutes, until the bird's juices run clear when you stick a knife into the fold between its thigh and its body and the potatoes have become lightly golden and crisp.

Ice Cream with Milky Way Sauce

There is nothing that is sophisticated and absolutely everything that is utterly delicious about this dessert. By some kind of alchemy, the Milky Way bar melts into a wonderfully delicate chocolate and caramel sauce, to which I like to add just a pinch of salt, to round the edge off the sweetness. The toasted sliced almonds on top are by no means necessary, and do skip them if you like, but I love the buttery crunch that they add.

HANDS ON TIME:
5 minutes
SERVES 1

½ standard-sized (1.84oz)
   Milky Way bar
2 tbsp heavy cream
1 tbsp sliced almonds
2 scoops of vanilla
   ice cream
flaky sea salt

Chop the Milky Way bar into small pieces and throw it into a small saucepan. Pour in the cream and warm gently over a low heat, stirring constantly until the chocolate is completely melted. This should take 3–4 minutes. Add a generous pinch of salt to taste.

In a second, non-stick frying pan, toast the sliced almonds until lightly golden.

Scoop the ice cream into a bowl. Pour the hot chocolate sauce over the ice cream, sprinkle over the almonds and eat immediately.

Baked Apple with Amaretti Crumble

✿ Package up in an airtight container or a small foil roasting pan with instructions to reheat, covered, in a medium oven, until warmed through.

I adore baked apples, most especially in the winter months when there is something so deeply nourishing as well as soothing about the warm, mellow fruit, so tender you can slice it with your spoon. Especially if I've had a light-ish something for dinner – a salad, for example – it can be nice to finish off on a warming note. You could just bake an apple as is: core it, then fill it with raisins, dates, some crystallized ginger if you like, and a drizzle of honey, and bake it. And when I want something plainer that's what I do, but when I'm craving something special and spoiling, this amaretti crumble hits the spot like nothing else.

HANDS ON TIME:
10 minutes
HANDS OFF TIME:
40–45 minutes in the oven
SERVES 1

3 amaretti cookies
2 tsp all-purpose flour
2 tsp turbinado sugar
½ tbsp salted butter, chilled
   and cut into small pieces
1 tbsp raisins
1 apple, preferably Gala
dollop of crème fraîche,
   whipped cream or
   vanilla ice cream,
   to serve (optional)

Heat the oven to 400°F.

Crumble the cookies into a mixing bowl and add the flour, sugar and butter. Work the mixture with your fingers until you have a crumble, then stir in the raisins.

Cut the top off the apple and scoop out the core with a spoon.

Spoon the crumble into the apple, making sure to cover any raisins with a little crumble. Scrunch a sheet of foil up, then nestle the apple on it and set in a roasting pan. Bake for 20 minutes without its top, then press the apple top over the crumble and set back in the oven for a further 20–25 minutes, until it feels tender to the touch.

Serve warm, perhaps with a dollop of crème fraîche, whipped cream or vanilla ice cream to go with it.

Apricot and Ginger Snap Cheesecake Quick Fix

✄ *Spoon into an old-fashioned glass and cover with reusable food wrap or parchment paper tied with twine; or store in a glass jar and seal with its lid. This will keep happily for two or three days in the fridge.*

When apricots are in season, you can make this with fresh fruit: just throw in a few slices of sweet, juicy apricot in place of the preserves prescribed below. But for the rest of the year, I use preserves, which gives a glorious hit of sugary sweetness against the sharpness of the cream cheese. By the same principle, you can happily make this with whatever preserves take your fancy: black cherry, orange marmalade, raspberry, strawberry, even rhubarb (either preserves or a few pieces of the fruit, hot-pink and tender, roasted or poached)... all work beautifully with the gingery heat of the crumbled cookies.

HANDS ON TIME:
10 minutes
SERVES 1

½ tbsp salted butter
3 ginger snap cookies
1 tsp granulated sugar
2 heaping tbsp cream cheese
2 heaping tbsp plain whole milk yogurt
1 heaping tbsp confectioners' sugar
1 heaping tbsp apricot preserves

Melt the butter in a small saucepan over a gentle heat. Crumble the cookies as finely as you can into the pool of melted butter, then add the granulated sugar and stir to combine. Spoon the gingery rubble into a glass.

Using a spoon, beat the cream cheese and yogurt together in a small bowl, add the confectioners' sugar and beat again until creamy and smooth.

Spoon the preserves over the layer of crumble, then top with the cream cheese mixture.

Chill in the fridge until you're ready to eat it.

Bitter Orange, Raisin and Rosemary Bread Pudding

✻ *Drop off in its ramekin (covered with reusable food wrap or parchment paper tied with twine) with instructions to reheat, covered, in a medium oven until warmed through. It will keep in the fridge for two or three days, or you could happily freeze it.*

This is a bread pudding just for one, only I use stale pain aux raisins in place of bread, then layer it with bitter orange marmalade and just a hint of rosemary (and no butter). The addition of the rosemary just rounds off the edges, so it's in no way sickly sweet, instead warming and somehow rather calming. It gives me that same happy feeling as a walk though the park on a cold, but piercingly bright day. And, like all bread puddings, it is deeply comforting to eat. If you can't find pain aux raisins, use a large croissant and 1 tbsp raisins instead.

HANDS ON TIME:
10 minutes
HANDS OFF TIME:
5–10 minutes resting;
25–30 minutes in the oven
SERVES 1

1 large pain aux raisins
    (roughly 4oz)
1 heaping tbsp orange
    marmalade
⅓ tsp finely chopped
    rosemary leaves
2 tbsp milk
2 tbsp heavy cream, plus
    more if needed, and
    (optional) to serve
1 egg yolk
¾ tbsp granulated sugar

Heat the oven to 325°F.

Cut up the pain aux raisins. Arrange half the pieces snugly in a small ovenproof dish (I use a 4-inch ramekin). Spoon over the marmalade and use the back of a spoon to spread it out evenly. Sprinkle over the chopped rosemary and top with the rest of the pastry.

Pour the milk and cream into a small saucepan and bring near to boiling point: you should see small bubbles form at the edge of the pan. In a small bowl or cup, whisk the yolk and sugar together with a fork, then pour into the warmed cream and keep whisking all the while.

Pour the warmed eggy cream into the ramekin, over the pain aux raisins, and leave to soak for 5–10 minutes. If there looks like there's space in the dish, then pour in a little more cream.

Bake in the oven for 25–30 minutes, until the custard is softly set. Serve warm, with a little cream, if you like.

Sourdough Toast with Bittersweet Chocolate and Olive Oil

I remember the first time I ate this: huddled at the bar at Prune in New York's East Village with my friend Douglas. We waxed lyrical about this dessert: its sheer simplicity and its sheer deliciousness. Chocolate on bread is of course a timelessly good combination, but it's the addition of a generous glug of olive oil and just a dash of flaky salt that elevates this above and beyond an improvised snack and into the lofty realms of dream desserts.

HANDS ON TIME:
5 minutes
SERVES 1

1 thick slice of sourdough
  bread
1oz good-quality
  (minimum 70 per
  cent cocoa solids)
  bittersweet chocolate,
  finely chopped (about
  2 tbsp)
olive oil
flaky sea salt

Toast the bread so that it's warmed through and nicely browned on both sides.

Top with the chocolate, drizzle with olive oil and sprinkle over a generous pinch of flaky salt.

Eat immediately.

MENUS

Here are a few ideas for occasions when
some of these recipes would be welcome.

MENUS FOR ONE

A soul-soothing dinner after
a long day
Penne with Saffron Cream (p.289)
Bitter Orange, Raisin and Rosemary
    Bread Pudding (p.305)

A quick fix for instant gratification
Arugula, Almond and Date Salad (p.270)
A few slivers of good hard cheese and/or
    some charcuterie
Ice Cream with Milky Way Sauce (p.298)

For when you're in the mood
for a proper meal
Roast Cornish Hen with Lemon Potatoes
    (p.297)
Green salad with olive oil, lemon and salt
Apricot and Ginger Snap Cheesecake Quick
    Fix (p.302)

Solo picnic in the park
(with a good book)
Black Rice, Roasted Garlic and Green Olive
    Salad, in an airtight box (p.278)
A few crunchy, peppery radishes with salt and
    butter for dipping
A punnet of strawberries with a small pot of
    heavy cream

Something warming for a
cold winter night
Baked Eggs with Spinach and Gorgonzola
    (p.274)
A nice chunk of good bread
Baked Apple with Amaretti Crumble (p.301)

When you need a treat
Fried Mozzarella Balls (p.280)
Cherry tomato salad, dressed with a drizzle of
    olive oil, a few basil leaves, salt and pepper
Ice Cream with Milky Way Sauce (p.298)

When you need a treat
(but are pressed for time)
Saltata di Risotto (p.294)
A nice salad of bitter endive leaves
Sourdough Toast with Bittersweet Chocolate
    and Olive Oil (p.306)

When your body is craving
healthy nourishment
Spinach and Lemon Soup (p.266)
Salmon en Papillote (p.293)
A few green salad leaves, lightly dressed with
    olive oil and salt
A bowl of cherries

MENUS FOR TWO

Brunch for the morning after
Black Truffle and Cheese Omelet (p.116)
Bryony's Clear Bloody Mary (p.92)
Buttered toast

Lazy breakfast in bed
Anthony's Special Crêpes with lemon and
    sugar (p.118)
Greek yogurt with mixed berries
A Moka of strong coffee

Dinner to impress on a first date
Scallops with Buttery Brandy Gratin
    (p.100)
Roast Duck Legs with Winter Citrus
    (p.111)
Orange, Beet and Feta Salad (p.112)
Nutella Tiramisù (p.123)

A Valentine's dinner
A Very Sexy Cocktail (p.91)
Fusilli with Lardo, Almonds and
   Honey (p.95)
Buttery Mackerel with Roasted
   Rhubarb (p.108)
Flourless Chocolate and Espresso Cakes
   with a few raspberries (p.135)

A (vegetarian) Valentine's dinner
A Very Sexy Cocktail (p.91)
Orange, Beet and Feta Salad (p.112)
Rhubarb and Cheddar Tart (p.99)
A nice salad of pink radicchio leaves, dressed
   with a little olive oil, lemon and salt
Chocolate and Rosemary Tart (p.124)

**A deliciously indulgent dinner
   (on a cold night)**
Some charcuterie to nibble on with a glass
   of prosecco
Cheese and Marmite Soufflé (p.104)
Baked potatoes and a crisp green salad
Toblerone Fondue (p.131)

**A deliciously indulgent dinner
   (on a balmy summer's evening)**
Some grissini and cheeses to nibble on with
   a glass of prosecco
Fregola Sarda with Seafood (p.115)
A crisp green salad
White Chocolate and Pistachio Tortini
   (p.136)

A simple, make-ahead menu
Roasted Dorade with Fennel and Tomatoes;
   prep everything in the roasting pan ahead
   of time, chill, then put in the oven when
   you're ready to go (p.103)
Boiled fingerling potatoes, dressed with olive
   oil, parsley and salt (made ahead of time
   and served at room temperature)
Baileys Pannacotta (p.128)

MENUS FOR FOUR
(OR MORE)

For when you need supper in a hurry
Pasta alla Bibi (p.148)
Yogurt and fresh fruit

**A deliciously effortless, make-ahead
   supper (and a solid picnic menu)**
Tomato, Mozzarella and Black Olive Tart
   (p.160) **OR** Red Bell Pepper and Feta
   Frittata (p.159)
Fava Beans with Feta and Almonds
   (p.181)
Strawberries with whipped cream
Salted Chocolate Chip Cookies (p.78)

**A family dinner you can cook together
   (children and all)**
Bread Pizza (p.165)
Cucumber chunks, dressed with a little olive
   oil, fresh mint and salt
Chocolate Chunk Bundt Cake (p.198)

A lazy Sunday dinner
Honey Roasted Chicken Thighs with Golden
   Potatoes (p.166)
Golden Crisp Leeks (p.182)
Baked Fennel and Burrata Gratin (p.37)
Sugared Plum Pudding (p.185)

Pure comfort and joy
Polpette alla Ricotta with Tomato Sauce
   (p.168), with good, crusty bread for
   mopping up the tomato juices
Buttered spinach
Ciocolatissimo Brownies (p.253)

**When you're too tired to cook and
   everyone is being picky**
Perfect Eggs on Toast (p.154)
A tomato salad with olive oil, salt and pepper
Yogurt with raspberries and nonpareils

A good solid meal

Pollo alla Pizzaiola (p.174)

Peas with a bit of salted butter and mint

Golden Crisp Leeks (p.182) **OR** A crisp
    green salad (or both)

Pistachio and Fig Queen of Puddings (p.76)

When craving greens and goodness

Pasta with Pesto and Extra Greens (p.146)

Vanilla ice cream (store-bought) with fresh fruit

MENUS FOR SIX
(OR MORE)

A birthday afternoon tea party

Egg sandwiches

Cheese sandwiches

Fairy bread (small squares of soft,
    buttered white bread, covered
    in nonpareils)

Aunt Effie's Oat Bars (p.201)

Fresh fruit

Birthday Cake of Dreams (p.194)

An unconventional Thanksgiving dinner

Soul-Soothing Roast Chicken (p.43)

Buttery Mashed Potatoes with Preserved
    Lemon (p.55)

Pumpkin and Mascarpone Flan (p.38)

Golden Crisp Leeks (p.182)

Sweet Potato and Marshmallow Pie (p.189)

**For when the world is falling apart
    around you**

Elle's Mac and Cheese (p.50)

A crisp green salad

Decadently Dark No-Churn Chocolate Ice
    Cream (p.75) with crumbled Salted
    Chocolate Chip Cookies (p.78), and
    whipped cream, to make ice cream sundaes

A birthday treat

A Very Good Chicken Salad (p.44)

Mustardy Potato Salad (p.56)

Fava Beans with Feta and Almonds (p.181)

Torta alla Meringata, with birthday candles
    (p.70)

Sunday supper with people you love

Petra's Creamy Saffron Chicken Pie (p.46)

Buttery Mashed Potatoes with Preserved
    Lemon (p.55)

Buttered Peas with a little fresh mint

Salted Caramel Apple Crumble (p.68)

A party just because

Maria's Many Cheese Tiropita (p.27)

A good tomato salad with black olives and
    fresh basil

Fava Beans with Feta and Almonds (p.181)

More S'mores Pie (p.64) **OR** Chocolate,
    Coconut and Cherry Cake (p.63)

A perfect picnic

A Very Good Chicken Salad (p.44)

A loaf of Date and Rosemary Soda Bread
    (p.240), already sliced

Quail's eggs with celery salt for dipping

Some good hard cheeses

Berry Crumble Cake (p.197)

**For when you need to cheer
    someone up**

Soul-Soothing Roast Chicken (p.43)

Golden Crisp Leeks (p.182)

A nice green salad

Baked Fennel and Burrata Gratin (p.37)

Salted Caramel Apple Crumble (p.68),
    with cream or ice cream

INDEX

A

almonds
    arugula, almond and date salad 270
    fava beans with feta and almonds 181
    fusilli with lardo, almonds and honey 95
    orange loaf cake 193
    panforte 250
    pistachio pesto 220
    rhubarb and almond cake 190
amaretti cookies
    baked apple with amaretti crumble 301
    berry crumble cake 197
anchovies: bread pizza 165
Anthony's special crêpes 118–19
apples
    baked apple with amaretti crumble 301
    pomegranate jelly 224
    salted caramel apple crumble 68
apricot, walnut and halloumi salad 269
apricot and ginger snap cheesecake quick fix 302
arugula
    apricot, walnut and halloumi salad 269
    arugula, almond and date salad 270
asparagus: salmon en papillote 293

Aunt Effie's oat bars 201

B

Baileys pannacotta 128
beets
    beet, walnut and Gorgonzola tart 28–9
    orange, beet and feta salad 112
bell peppers: bell pepper and feta frittata 159
berry crumble cake 197
birthday cake of dreams 194
Bloody Mary, Bryony's clear 92
brandy
    brandy butter 249
    rhubarb syllabub 127
    scallops with buttery brandy gratin 100
    spiced oranges with brandy and sugar 132
bread
    bread pizza 165
    date and rosemary soda bread 240
    polpette alla ricotta with tomato sauce 168–9
    sourdough toast with bittersweet chocolate
        and olive oil 306

bread pudding, bitter orange, raisin and
    rosemary 305
brioche: sugared plum pudding 185
broccoli: pasta with pesto and extra greens 146
brownies, ciocolatissimo 253
Bryony's clear Bloody Mary 92
bundt cake, chocolate chunk 198
burrata: baked fennel and burrata gratin 37
butter
    brandy butter 249
    buttery mackerel with roasted rhubarb 108
    buttery mashed potatoes, preserved lemon 55
buttermilk: date and rosemary soda bread 240

C

cakes
    berry crumble cake 197
    birthday cake of dreams 194
    Certosino Christmas cake 243
    chocolate, coconut and cherry cake 63
    chocolate chunk bundt cake 198
    ciocolatissimo brownies 253
    Delilah cake 256–7
    flourless chocolate and espresso cakes 135
    lavender and raisin tea cake 230–1
    orange loaf cake 193
    raspberry and marzipan cake 254
    rhubarb and almond cake 190
Campari: a very sexy cocktail 91
candied peel: panforte 250
cantucci, chocolate and hazelnut 239
capers
    pollo alla pizzaiola 174
    tonno alla filicudara 173
caramel: salted caramel apple crumble 68
Certosino Christmas cake 243
cheese
    apricot, walnut and halloumi salad 269
    baked eggs with spinach and Gorgonzola 274
    baked fennel and burrata gratin 37
    beet, walnut and Gorgonzola tart 28–9
    black truffle and cheese omelet 116
    bread pizza 165
    cheese and Marmite soufflé 104
    effortless *melanzane alla Parmigiana* 176–7
    Elle's mac and cheese 50–1
    fava beans with feta and almonds 181
    fried mozzarella balls 280–1
    Maria's many cheese tiropita 27
    orange, beet and feta salad 112
    pasta with pesto and extra greens 146
    pollo alla pizzaiola 174

ACKNOWLEDGMENTS

Through the process of writing this book
– long, rambling and occasionally bumpy as
it's been – I've been touched by the passion
that everyone has shown the project; and the
love that they've shown me along the way.
Try as I might, I struggle to find words that
accurately convey how deeply and forever
grateful I am to each and every one of you
who has helped me create these pages I am so
proud of: in the absence of the perfect thing to
say, here are a few words of thanks. It's by no
means enough, but I hope goes some way in
expressing how grateful I feel...

To Caroline Michel, for always fighting my
corner, showing such inexhaustible passion
for each of my books and for supporting me
every step of the way. Thank you: I couldn't
wish for a better agent or friend.

To Laura Creyke and Mark Hutchinson,
for always being such a steadfast support,
and for being the very best at what you do. As
ever, it's sheer joy working with you.

To my wonderful editor, Rowan Yapp, for
getting behind this idea of a-cookbook-that-
isn't-really-about-food from the get-go, mad
as it sounded; and for supporting me so
wholeheartedly to create the book that I had
long dreamed about. It has been a pleasure
and a privilege to get to know you better
while working on this book together and
I have loved every moment of it. Huge thanks
also to all the Bloomsbury team for your
tireless hard work and boundless enthusiasm;
most especial thanks to Lena Hall, Rose
Brown, Ellen Williams and Laura Brodie
in Production. And, of course, to Greg
Heinimann for designing a cover that I love.
In the American Bloomsbury office, thank
you to Lauren Ollerhead and Marie
Coolman in publicity; Lauren Dooley and
Lauren Mosely in marketing, Valentina Rice,
and my US editor, Harriet LaFavour.

I'd also love to thank Caroline Stearns, for
her rigorous Americanization work.

To Clare Baggaley, for designing these
pages so exquisitely. Thank you for taking on
the challenge of a rambling brief with such
warmth and energy, and then working it into
a book that is more beautiful and more perfect
than anything I could ever have imagined.

To Stephanie Howard for capturing each
and every one of the beautiful images where
I'm in the shot and not behind the camera,
and for assisting me with the rest of the
photography. You have such a talent for
finding the magic light and for capturing those
quiet, unexpected and beautiful moments. I am
forever grateful for your tireless hard work on
this book, most especially when you were
expecting, and I've loved every moment.

To Ellie Mulligan for cooking the most
beautiful food to grace these pages: you can
make even the humblest of things (and the
brownest of dishes) look utterly dreamy; but
above all, thank you for being so much fun.
Huge thanks also to Toni Musgrave, Kristine
Jakobsson and Maria Gurevich for all your
invaluable help in the kitchen.

To Poppy Mahon, for unflagging hard
work testing the recipes and making sure
they work perfectly; then going back and
testing them again. Thank you for going
above and beyond and for being such a
trooper, working to a very tight timeframe.
I would be lost without you; and this would
have been a lesser cookbook without you.

To Lucy Bannell, for bringing these pages
together so beautifully and so punctiliously.
Your eye for detail, and the rigor with which
you approach each task, is forever inspiring;
but thank you above all for your warmth and
energy, for being so patient and understanding
about my chaotic way of working, and for
being so unreservedly generous – always –
with your time and feedback.

To Richard Atkinson, my most patient
and generous friend, for the hours you spent
helping me to make sense of my thoughts and

pushing me to write them down. Thank you for always being so generous with your time, your wisdom, and enthusiasm; for being so honest with your feedback; and for always believing that I could do this.

To my Mama, so many of the recipes among the pages here are yours. You cooked them for me and taught me how to cook them for myself, just as you've taught me so much of what I live my life by today. Thank you.

To my boys, Anthony, Aeneas and Achille, for believing in me, loving me and for reminding me why it is that I do what I do.

And last, but by no means least, the biggest thank you to all my friends who have contributed to this book by sharing recipes, thoughts, friendship and encouragement along the way. Most special thanks to Elle Chadwick, Stella Powell-Jones, Sue Gilkes, Delilah Khomo, Carolyn Asome and Hugo MacDonald. And to my darling Bryony Rae Sheridan for the hours you have spent plotting and planning with me, going over the recipes again and again, and cheering me along when I crashed into the rock-hard wall that is writer's block.

BLOOMSBURY PUBLISHING
Bloomsbury Publishing Inc.
1385 Broadway, New York, NY 10018, USA

BLOOMSBURY, BLOOMSBURY PUBLISHING, and
the Diana logo are trademarks of Bloomsbury Publishing Plc.

First published in Great Britain 2023
First published in the United States of America 2023

Text © Skye McAlpine, 2023
Photographs © Skye McAlpine, 2023

Library of Congress Cataloging-in-Publication Data
is available.

ISBN: HB: 978-1-63973-049-0
eBook: 978-1-63973-050-6

10 9 8 7 6 5 4 3 2 1

Project Editor: Lucy Bannell
Designer: Clare Baggaley
Photographer: Skye McAlpine
Assistant Photographer: Stephanie Howard
Food Stylist: Eleanor Mulligan
Indexer: Vanessa Bird

Printed and bound in China by C&C Offset Printing Ltd.

To find out more about our authors and books visit
www.bloomsbury.com and sign up for our newsletters.

Bloomsbury books may be purchased for business or
promotional use. For information on bulk purchases
please contact Macmillan Corporate and Premium Sales
Department at specialmarkets@macmillan.com.

SKYE MCALPINE is a cookery
writer who believes that food tastes best
when shared with others. She is the
author of two books, *A Table in Venice*
and *A Table for Friends*. In 2021 she
launched her own curated range of
homeware, Skye McAlpine TAVOLA.
She divides her time between London
and Venice with her husband, Anthony,
and two sons, Aeneas and Achille.